THE SECOND
WORLD WAR
IN COLOUR

THE SECOND WORLD WAR
IN COLOUR

--

STEWART BINNS
AND ADRIAN WOOD

FOREWORD BY
SIR LUDOVIC KENNEDY

PAVILION

DEDICATION

This book is dedicated to Lucy Binns and Cath Wood, our partners in life, who make it all worthwhile. It is also written in admiration of and out of respect for all those who died, suffered and survived the Second World War in their fight for freedom.

First published in Great Britain in 1999 by PAVILION BOOKS LIMITED
London House, Great Eastern Wharf,
Parkgate Road, London SW11 4NQ

A TWI Production for Carlton © Carlton Television Limited 1999

Designed by Nigel Partridge

A CIP catalogue record for this book is available from the British Library.

ISBN 1 86205 349 9

Set in New Baskerville and Futura

Colour reproduction by Colourpath, London
Printed and bound in Italy by Conti Tipocolor

1 3 5 7 9 10 8 6 4 2

This book may be ordered by post direct from the publisher.
Please contact the Marketing Department. But try your bookshop first.

HALF-TITLE PAGE: A Canadian fighter pilot of No 417 Squadron, RCAF climbs into the cockpit of his Spitfire at Goubrine airfield during the campaign in the Tunisian Desert, May 1943.

TITLE PAGE: A German soldier writes in 1941 from the Eastern Front.

CONTENTS

FOREWORD

Unless one is colour blind, we humans see life in colour: therefore all images on film presented in black and white are distortions of what is observed.

Historically we had to make do with black and white for a long time, for although some American movies were first made in colour before the war, it was not until comparatively recently that technology allowed newspapers to introduce colour printing.

During the war I do not recall seeing any Pathé, Movietone or Gaumont British newsreels in colour, and when I was serving in a destroyer and a newsreel agency sent me some rolls of film to use in a friend's borrowed cine camera, there was no question of them being in other than black and white. Also in black and white were the latest feature films sent by the Royal Naval Film Corporation for the entertainment of ships' companies in desolate anchorages such as Scapa Flow. Finally, when I came to make a series of documentary films for the BBC on the German navy's participation in the war, none of their archive material (despite stocks of Agfa) or ours was in colour. Film images of my war, therefore, and that of my companions, was exclusively black and white.

Thus the colour pictures in this book have come as a revelation to me, for film shot in colour makes a much greater impact and shows many more details than the same thing in black and white. Take the stark picture on page 199 of the single, semi-destroyed building standing alone in the wasteland that was Hiroshima after the dropping of the atomic bomb. The rubble in the foreground with its different shades of brown, grey and pale blue emphasises what is lacking in the flatness of the black and white, that many fine buildings in a variety of colour shades once stood here, and this is all that remains. The same is true of the horrifying photograph of Mussolini and his mistress Clara Petacci, newly killed by Italian partisans. I remember being shocked when I first saw this picture in black and white soon after it was taken. The shock is even greater when seen in colour, the marks on Mussolini's shirt which in black and white could be taken as smudges of dirt, are now clearly shown to be his blood.

It is mostly in the colour prints taken in repose rather than in action that we see for the first time the details that are invisible in black and white. Look at the posed photograph, presumably for publicity purposes, of the famous bomber pilot, Guy Gibson, at ease with a book in a field of poppies (page 131). Colour is the whole point of this photograph; without colour it would be nothing. Clearly the choice of the poppy field was to create a resonance with that earlier war on the Western Front. Then observe the medal ribbons on Gibson's chest, impossible to identify in black and white; the Victoria Cross, DSO and Bar, DFC and Bar, are tokens that bear witness to one man's exceptional skills and bravery.

Again in the picture on page 49 of the Spitfire pilot being treated to a short back and sides between sorties against the Luftwaffe, we see what we can't see in black and white: the title and author of the book he is reading – *Greenmantle* by John Buchan. And a third example of how colour heightens definition is to be seen on page 23 of Hitler's tea party at his mountain residence of the Berghof; what one would barely notice in black and white is (unless I am mistaken) a dainty glass of sherry beside the monster's plate.

The more I look at some of these colour prints, the more I find there is to see in them, in particular the aftermath of German air raids. On page 59 the thick, black smoke from burning oil tanks contrasts tellingly with the tranquillity of the local cemetery, while on page 71, a house with its outer wall peeled away juxtaposes with the top deck of a London bus, half buried in the rubble; and a similar graphic picture on page 60 of the ruins of Calais shows burnt out cars, an abandoned field gun and a derelict bicycle lying together in a jumble of destruction.

Even more graphic in the Far Eastern theatre is the picture of the doomed Japanese soldier flushed from his foxhole (page 157) and, silhouetted against the flame from the flame-throwers presumably thrown by the G.I. in the foreground; and there is something almost surreal in the picture on page 185 of some thirty-two Japanese mini-submarines, squatting like

wounded ducks in the remains of a huge, partially flooded dry dock.

Yet the picture which stays in my mind more than any other is that of the men of the American 92nd (Negro) Division on page 125, clearing mines from an Italian beach just before the end of the war. At this time the American army was racially segregated, (hence the use of the now discredited word Negro) many white Americans regarding their black fellow countrymen as inferior, a situation which, as the text admits, led to much racial tension. To me, the picture raises an awkward question. Did the white generals who employed these black soldiers on mine clearance do so because they were black and therefore expendable, or were there white mine-clearance units in Italy as well?

To be given the privilege of browsing through this unique set of World War Two colour pictures has been a great treat. My only regret is that there are not many more of them. Perhaps, hidden in lofts and attics, there are, and one day they also will see the light.

LUDOVIC KENNEDY
June 1999

INTRODUCTION

There is a widespread perception about the Second World War so pervasive that it has gone almost unchallenged for three generations. You will find it reflected in almost all the history books, and in most of the visual documentary and archival records of the war. At a profound and unconscious level it colours – or rather discolours – our memories of the events that took place between 1939 and 1945.

The perception is that the war was fought in black and white.

It must have been. That is how it has been presented for sixty years. The Second World War comes to us in shades of grey, drained of the hues of reality. 'The past is a foreign country: they do things differently there.'

Not so in contemporary coverage of war and ethnic cleansing, like that of Slobodan Milosevic's campaign against the Kosovan Albanians and the Bosnian Muslims. The TV news pictures showing vivid colour evidence of torture and mass killings have reminded the world of the terrible legacy of Hitler's Holocaust which we hoped and prayed could never be repeated.

And yet the post-Second World War generations have been strangely cushioned from the reality of that war; spared the gruesome awfulness of the full-colour portrayal of modern wars.

In this book we have tried to refresh our historical imagination so that the past can be brought back into the present, both in true colour pictures and by the words of those who experienced the harsh reality of war. What follows is a selection of writings of those who witnessed the war. Their testament is accompanied by a brief narrative of the events of the war, illustrated by some of the many thousands of colour photographs, most previously unpublished, which reflect the colour of war as seen by the pioneers of colour photography and cinematography. All of these pictures are unique and valuable.

In recent years the vast majority of TV programme makers have shared in the preconceptions of society as a whole that the Second World War was a 'black and white war', so that much of the colour footage which has survived remained in archives, unseen and forgotten.

Finding new or unpublished material from the war is not difficult. But it involves diligence and persistence.

BELOW: Jack Havener, a Marauder bomber pilot with the 344th Bomb Group of the 9th USAAF, in his billet at Stanstead, mid-1944, reading the US magazine Air Force.

ABOVE: Children play in the liberated ruins of Sicily, 15 August 1943.

Like all detective work the rewards are hugely satisfying. There is still film to be found, even in colour. There must be hundreds of colour photographs lying undiscovered in attics and archives. There are countless letters and diaries waiting to be read. They lie in national archives, military museums, local libraries, private collections and in innumerable homes all over the world.

With the invention of still photography and moving pictures, the world was able to see itself for the first time, though at first only in black and white. Photographs were used to 'document' events from the 1840s through the use of daguerreotypes.[1] *The Illustrated London News*, begun in May 1842, and *L'Illustration*, launched in Paris in March 1843, owe their origins to the invention of photography. The use of wet plates from 1851 made instant exposure possible.[2] Images of major historical events, notably Matthew Brady's photographs of the American Civil War in the 1860s, could be shown to mass audiences. Dry plates followed in 1871 and in 1889 the Eastman Kodak Company produced the first celluloid film.[3,4] At each stage, images of the world became easier to produce, more economical and an increasingly important part of our lives.

The arrival of the 'motion picture' at the end of the nineteenth century made images of the world even more significant elements of our culture. Various techniques to re-create motion had been used for a number of years, including 'magic-lantern' tricks created by a revolving drums of images, Edward Muybridge's pictures in motion and Etienne-Jules Marey's photographic rifle.[5,6,7] But it wasn't until Thomas Edison's patent of the kinetograph, and the Lumière brothers' perfecting of it, that motion pictures became accurate, authentic representations of reality.[8] The Lumières' film, shot in 1895, of *Workers Leaving the Lumière Factory* became the first documentary film of unstaged real life.

Thus, still photographs and moving images became key historical documents. The Boer War was the first to be recorded on moving film, in 1900, by news photographer and film-maker Joseph Rosenthal. By the 1930s, documentaries and cinema newsreels had become important expressions of social comment and propaganda. Directors such as Robert Flaherty (*Nanook of the North*, New York, 1922), John Grierson (*The Drifters*, London, 1929), Jean Vigo (*À propos de Nice*, 1930) and Leni Riefenstahl (Nazi propaganda films *Triumph of the Will*, 1934 and *Olympia*, 1938) all realized the power to move people made possible by moving images of reality.

So it was with still photography. Picture magazines like *Münchner Illustrierte Zeitung* in Germany, *Vu* in France, *Picture Post* in Britain and *Life* in America began to use photographs as part of the journalistic style of

9

the publication. Photographers were encouraged to 'interpret' scenes; their work thus took on a message and a meaning.

However, almost all this powerful imagery was presented in black and white. Although colour techniques were available from the 1900s, they were fraught with difficulties brought about by technical problems and high levels of cost. Initially, black and white images were hand-painted to replicate the real world. Other techniques included tinting[9] and toning[10] and Kinemacolor[11] and Kodacolor[12].

The real breakthrough came in the 1930s. Hollywood films began to be shot in Technicolor from as early as 1925 with *The Black Prince*, starring Douglas Fairbanks. Although Technicolor, a high-quality, highly expensive 35mm technique, was too elaborate for newsreels and documentaries, the German company Agfa introduced Gasparcolor in 1931, the first widely available single-roll colour negative film. In 1935 Kodachrome was launched into the American market by Eastman Kodak. These two film stocks enabled the first widespread use of colour film.

Almost the entire colour record of the Second World War, from a parade of Nazis in 1933 to the Japanese surrender in 1945, was shot on one of these stocks. But there were still problems: in projecting colour film, in printing it in newspapers and magazines, in finding colour stock during the deprivations of war and in gaining acceptance of the often shocking reality of colour. For these reasons, most of it has remained unseen until very recently.

When *Life* magazine published colour photographs in August 1944, they felt the need to print an editorial comment to accompany the images taken by photographer George Silk:

These pictures also show that ordinary black and white photographs have not done full descriptive justice to the war in Italy. They have omitted the soft

ABOVE: A German Army Propaganda Company films the ruins of Dunkirk and abandoned equipment of the British Expeditionary Force (BEF) after its capture on 4 June 1940.

RIGHT: An American M4 Sherman tank on an exercise at the Edgewood Arsenal in the US in 1943. Coloured smoke was used to identify individual targets and positions including their own. It was invaluable in reducing casualties from 'friendly fire'.

browns and grays of the ruined Italian towns, the bright shocking redness of freshly spilled blood, the incongruously gay colour of spring in the midst of battle.

The German magazine *Signal* was produced under the control of Joseph Goebbels' Propaganda Ministry. It had no qualms about colour, nor about its propaganda value. In 1943 its circulation reached 2.5 million and one-third of its photographs were in colour. However, Germany didn't make extensive use of colour in official documentary films, except for special events like Hitler visiting Bückeburg. The majority of documentaries were

produced, as elsewhere in the world, in black and white. But, a few German citizens, who had seen a large increase in their disposable income since Adolf Hitler took power in 1931, did use colour. Many of the images in the television series that this book accompanies are drawn from amateur film-makers who could afford colour film. Germany did introduce the occasional newsreel, later in the war. *Panorama* was a propaganda production, designed to reinforce German morale, despite Allied assaults on all fronts. Its output included scenes from northern Italy and anti-submarine patrols off Norway.

The Soviet Union also produced some colour film, again from the late 1930s. The first documentary in colour was of the 1938 Sport Parade in Red Square with, not surprisingly, Stalin in the central role. Between the 1938 parade and the same event in 1945 (attended by US General Eisenhower), the Soviet Union produced only seven colour films which can be traced today.

America was by far the largest consumer of colour film. Colour had been relatively widely used in educational and training films before the outbreak of war. As early as 1930, the US Navy had encouraged *National*

Geographic magazine to collaborate with Eastman Kodak and the US Army Air Corps on an aerial photography project. The initial use of colour film in government documentaries was in the production of military training films. It was believed that dull subjects would be enlivened if presented in colour. It was also valuable in the production of medical training films, ammunition recognition training and in camouflage assessment, where colour was vital for identification.

Many of the film units operating in the US armed forces during the war were headed by well-known Hollywood directors such as Darryl Zanuck, John Ford, John Huston, William Wyler and George Stevens. Stevens was responsible for much of the filming of events in Europe from D-Day to VE Day. Principally shooting in black and white, he also exposed colour film for his own personal record. This personal material and John Ford's official footage greatly influenced Steven Spielberg's *Saving Private Ryan*. More and more colour began to be used towards the end of the war. The 1944 US Navy production *The Fighting Lady*, the story of an aircraft carrier task force in the Pacific, was so highly praised that it prompted the United States Army Air Force (USAAF) to initiate special Kodachrome film projects in Europe, as well as in the Pacific theatre.

One of the most acclaimed productions from the European arena was William Wyler's *Memphis Belle* (1943), chronicling a mission of a B-17 Flying Fortress on a daylight raid over Wilhelmshaven, Germany. It was made using actual footage shot over the combat zone, but compiled from five separate missions.

The British Government's Ministry of Information rarely used colour film for its productions. One exception was *Western Approaches*, directed by Pat Jackson for the Crown Film Unit. Using scenes shot from North Atlantic convoys, inter-cut with Royal Navy personnel in their normal roles, the film tells the vital story of the German U-boat operations against merchant and Royal Navy shipping between the USA and Britain.

BELOW: Private photographs, such as this of Jack Havener, were not subject to censorship of items such as the invasion fleet in the harbour or secret radar antennae in the left background.

ABOVE: Members of British Army Film & Photographic Unit No. 2 at a briefing in Italy, 30 September 1943. The photographer, Len Chetwyn, ran AFPU NO. 2, which was nicknamed 'Chet's Circus'.

The various film and photographic units of the three British services used colour film much less than their American counterparts. A notable exception was footage shot with the British Army's Long Range Desert Group, precursor of the now famous SAS (Special Air Service), acting behind enemy lines in North Africa in 1942. While full written documentation from the army cameraman who shot it exists, the film itself has not been heard of since it was made. Like so many of the materials now being unearthed for the first time, it probably lies in a corner of some dusty attic.

Much of the colour material discovered over the past twenty years was still in the possession of those who shot it, or their descendants. One marvellous example is the collection of Rosie Newman. While in the WVS, she shot material in France during the last days of the Phoney War. Upon her return to England, with the assistance of influential friends in the government and the Armed

ABOVE: Lt H Aldridge of Surbiton Hill, Surrey, a member of the British 8th Army in Italy, reads a letter from home. At Lauro, in Italy, 19 January 1944.

RIGHT: A German soldier reads a letter in 1941 from the Eastern Front.

ABOVE: Two women take a pause from war on the Home Front and write letters in London's Hyde Park.

Forces, she was able to begin a filmed record of Britain at War. Ignoring censorship regulations and the desperate shortage of colour film, she captured an almost unique colour record of wartime Britain. Rosie Newman continued showing her films for charitable purposes after the war. Fortuitously, her collection was kept by her family and is now preserved by the Imperial War Museum in London.

Another interesting example is Göetz Hirt-Reger. He was a 21-year-old soldier in the German army as it advanced into the Soviet Union in Operation Barbarossa in 1941. At this stage he took amateur film, which his father managed to save from army confiscation. But the army, alerted to his skill, soon recruited him as a propaganda cameraman. He shot official material of the battles of Kursk and Orel, but continued to shoot his own private material, emphasizing the life of the ordinary soldier, much of which has survived.

The written material contained in the following chapters is drawn from numerous sources: national archives, regional and private archives and personal papers. It includes official memoranda and instructions, personal diary entries and letters from the battlefield. Despite wartime restrictions on diary-keeping by combatants, for fear of intelligence leaks if captured, many thousands of individuals in all services, from all the warring nations, recorded their personal thoughts. Although all correspondence between military personnel and civilians was heavily censored, the private fears, aspirations and emotions of ordinary soldiers were recorded.

Written in school notebooks, on scraps of salvaged paper, or even on cigarette papers in tiny writing, they preserved the testimony of the day, retaining the integrity of impressions that time often blurs.

(SEE P. 204 FOR FOOTNOTES.)

PART ONE

A NEW
WORLD ORDER

STORM CLOUDS GATHER

1933-39

The inevitability of the Second World War, from as early as 1933, now seems all too obvious with the benefit of two generations of hindsight. At the time, however, the horrors of the Great War were too recent and too vivid to permit reasonable people to do anything other than meet nationalism with containment and aggression with moderation. Although fascism was on the march in Europe, Japan was waging war in Asia and the Soviet Union was flexing the very considerable muscles of the new ideology of communism, the world shied away from confrontations with the reality of oppression and violence.

When Adolf Hitler became Chancellor of Germany in January 1933, it was both a beginning and an end. All too sadly, it was the beginning of a tragedy that would unfold on an epic scale over the following twelve years. It was a tragedy that would cost fifty million lives and leave a stain on the soul of humanity that may never be cleansed.

It was also the end of a chain of events caused by a less heinous, but equally prophetic, human folly: The Treaty of Versailles. Again with the benefit of hindsight, the price exacted at Versailles by the vengeful victors of the First World War was too great for Germany to bear. It left a tumour of resentment that grew inexorably into National Socialism. It nurtured the ambitions of a man who would bring a new dimension to the meaning of evil. In short, it rendered the peace that so many millions had fought for in the Great War into nothing more than an interlude before the suffering began

again; on an even greater scale and with an even greater loss of life.

But the scale of the tragedy was not the most significant difference between the two world wars. The Great War was a war between nations. It was fought for national interests; for power and for territory. The Second World War was fought between ideologies. It was fought for people's minds; for beliefs and for values. Ultimately, it became a struggle for freedom.

If, in 1919, the Treaty of Versailles created the political agenda of the inter-war years, then the Great Depression of 1929 shifted the economic agenda so that it too engendered the hardships and hostilities all too easily exploited by those with an ideological axe to grind. The spark provided by the Wall Street Crash led to an economic catastrophe. Unemployment escalated to two million in Britain, six million in Germany and fifteen million in the United States. Nations were led to engage in economic ruthlessness to protect themselves. The United States chose isolationism; Germany and Japan chose expansion.

Benito Mussolini was the first dictator to set the tone of the inter-war years. He became Italian Prime Minister as early as 1922 and *Il Duce* (the leader) in 1925. His charismatic style became a template for the leaders who would come to dominate the political theatre of the war. Each nation seemed to create its own cult of personality: Hitler, Stalin, Roosevelt, Churchill, de Gaulle, Tojo, Franco, Chiang Kai-Shek and Mao Tse Tung; all became the heroes of their cause.

ABOVE: Decorations on Berlin's Unter den Linden to mark Hitler's 50th birthday on 20 April 1939.

Mussolini's ambitions led to war in Ethiopia in 1935, and later, to territorial gains in North Africa. Ultimately, he became Hitler's ally in the south; for as long as it suited his purposes.

Francisco Franco's nationalist revolt in 1936, and the subsequent battle of ideologies that was the Spanish Civil War, provided a macabre overture for what was to follow four years later on a global scale. The bombing of Madrid and Guernica offered an awful premonition of the horrors to come.

Japan's ambition was more akin to old-fashioned territorial imperialism, based on economic avarice, than to the spread of an ideology. But its conquests threatened powerful interests. Its annexation of Manchuria in 1932 brought it into conflict with the Soviet Union. The invasion of China, in 1937, threatened European and Australasian interests on the Pacific rim. Ultimately, its expansion into the Pacific brought the might of America into the war and the frontline of the Pacific theatre to the beaches of California and Queensland.

Fascism toppled governments and generated turmoil in many countries: the Iron Guard in Romania, the Arrow Cross in Hungary, the Ustasas of Croatia and the Austrian Nazis. There were also vociferous adherents in Britain, France, Poland, Greece and Portugal. The traumas of the Depression made extremist ideologies attractive refuges for frightened people.

ABOVE: 'The idea of a greater Germany' had been dreamt about by German nationalists. By August 1939, it had been achieved.

Even in America domestic hardship produced hostility and violence as the unemployed and dispossessed struggled against forces they couldn't control. Perhaps the most telling outcome of American internal problems was its resultant unwillingness to become embroiled in external conflict until it exploded in its face at Pearl Harbor in 1941.

But the real marauding menace, that gave full rein to the dark forces at work in the 1930s, was Adolf Hitler and National Socialism. He was to create a truly evil empire like no other before, or since. Within a month of coming to power, he had taken advantage of the Reichstag fire, in which the building burned to the ground, and then used the crime as an excuse to suspend civil liberties. A year later, he murdered his ally Ernst Röhm, and many of his followers, and soon

became *Führer* (leader), after the death of President Hindenburg. Anti-Jewish legislation was fully in place by the end of 1935. In the spring of 1936, German troops re-occupied the demilitarized Rhineland.

None of these actions should have been a surprise. His ruthlessness was never in doubt; his intentions couldn't have been expressed more clearly than in *Mein Kampf,* his political manifesto, written in 1924. He believed in 'rule' not freedom, he was determined that those he defined as 'superior' should subjugate those he thought 'inferior', and he believed that his 'master race' had to have 'living space' (*Lebensraum*). He said,

'If we want to rule, we must first conquer Russia.'

The worthy but indecisive men who tried so hard to make appeasement work were toiling in vain. Germany marched into Austria in March 1938. British and French Prime Ministers, Chamberlain and Daladier, made one last futile attempt to treat with Hitler at Munich in September, and ceded the German-speaking Sudetenland in the process. It was, pathetically, to no avail. *Kristallnacht,* a night of organized Nazi looting and destruction of Jewish shops and property throughout Germany, followed in November 1938. German Jews finally saw Nazi terror in all its mighty fury and hatred.

BELOW: Hitler salutes a march-past of the SA in Nuremberg, Party Day, 1938. The last of the great Nazi rallies to be held there.

Hitler's impassioned pleas about protecting Germans in the Sudetenland was just a disguise. The *Wehrmacht,* the German armed forces, marched into the rest of Czechoslovakia in March 1939. Only Poland stood between the 'Master Race' and the 'living space' of Russia.

In the Soviet Union, a Bolshevik dictator had been perpetrating his own reign of terror for several years. While millions of people died in Stalin's purges, his evil empire secretly conspired with Hitler's National Socialism (two ideologies that were supposed to be the antithesis of one another), to dissect Poland and the Baltic. In a secret additional protocol of the Nazi–Soviet Pact of August 1939, the region was to be divided between the two empires. Stalin became another who didn't listen to, or chose to ignore, Hitler's clearly stated ambitions. Soon the tanks would roll from the West and the East.

19

JANUARY 1933–AUGUST 1939

1933

JAN. 30 Adolf Hitler is appointed Chancellor of Germany.

FEB. 9 In Britain, the Oxford Union Society supports the motion, 'that this house will in no circumstances fight for its King and its country'.

FEB. 23 The Japanese Imperial Army advances south from occupied Manchuria.

FEB. 27 Fire destroys the Reichstag. The Nazis claim a communist plot and suspend all civil liberties in Germany.

MAR. 4 Franklin Delano Roosevelt is inaugurated as US President. He says, 'The only thing we have to fear is fear itself.'

1934

FEB. 12 A general strike in France to protest at the rise of fascism.

JUNE 8 Oswald Mosley holds a mass rally of the British Union of Fascists in London.

JUNE 14 Benito Mussolini and Adolf Hitler meet for the first time in Venice.

JUNE 29/30 Ernst Röhm, head of the SA, and Hitler's closest political ally, and many of his followers are massacred by the SS on Hitler's order, in the 'Night of the Long Knives'.

JULY 25 Engelbert Dollfuss, Chancellor of Austria, is murdered in a Nazi coup attempt.

AUG. 2 President Hindenburg dies. Chancellor Hitler becomes supreme *Führer* of Germany.

1935

SEP. 15 Anti-Jewish legislation is outlined at the Nuremberg Rally. The Swastika becomes the German national flag.

OCT. 2 Italy invades Ethiopia.

1936

MAR. 7 German troops occupy the demilitarized Rhineland.

MAY 8 Italy annexes Ethiopia.

JULY 17 An army mutiny in Spanish Morocco, led by Francisco Franco, begins the Spanish Civil War.

OCT. 12 Oswald Mosley leads an anti-Jewish march through the East End of London.

NOV. 1 Mussolini proclaims the Rome–Berlin Axis.

1937

FEB. 27 France extends the Maginot Line, the defensive fortification along its border with Germany.

APR. 27 The German Condor Legion bombs Guernica in the Spanish Civil War.

JUNE 1 Stalin's terror campaign intensifies with a purge of the armed forces.

JULY 7 The Marco Polo Bridge 'incident' in Beijing leads to the Sino–Japanese War.

AUG. 8 Japan attacks Shanghai.

NOV. 8 A Nazi plot is discovered in Paris.

DEC. 5 During the 'Rape of Nanking' by the Japanese, 250,000 Chinese are killed.

1938

MAR. 13 *Anschluss*. Germany annexes Austria.

SEP. 29 Prime Ministers Neville Chamberlain and Edouard Daladier meet Hitler and Mussolini at the Munich Conference and agree to German occupation of the Sudetenland. Chamberlain and Hitler sign 'peace in our time' communiqué.

OCT. 25 Libya is declared part of Italy.

NOV. 9 *Kristallnacht*, a night of widespread attacks on synagogues and Jewish property throughout Germany.

1939

JAN. 26 Barcelona falls to Franco and the Nationalists.

MAR. 15 Hitler annexes Czechoslovakia and makes a triumphal entry into Prague.

MAR. 28 Madrid falls to Franco, the Spanish Civil War ends.

APR. 7 Italy invades Albania.

MAY 22 Mussolini and Hitler sign the 'Pact of Steel'.

AUG. 23 A Nazi–Soviet pact agrees a secret partition of Poland.

Nationalist Socialist principles stated that a hierarchy of races exists, with 'Aryans' at the top and Jews at the bottom. 'Aryan' was never precisely defined, but included the Germans, the English and the Scandinavians. Heinrich Himmler, a former chicken farmer, became the champion of racial purity as leader of the SS.

FRIDAY, 10 MARCH 1933 – VICTOR KLEMPERER

Klemperer was the son of a rabbi. In 1933 he was the Chair of Romance Languages and Literature at Dresden Technical University. Married to an Aryan German, Eva, he observed the continuing expansion of Nazi power.

DRESDEN, GERMANY

30th January: Hitler Chancellor. What, up to election Sunday on 5th March, I called terror, was a mild prelude. Now the business of 1918 is being exactly repeated, only under a different sign, under the swastika. Again it's astounding how easily everything collapses.

21

Eight days before the election the clumsy business of the Reichstag fire [Originally blamed on Communists, it is now known to have been the work of an anti-Nazi Dutch anarchist Marinus van der Lubbe] – I cannot imagine that anyone really believes in Communist perpetrators instead of paid Nazi work. Then the wild prohibitions and acts of violence. And on top of that the never-ending propaganda in the street, on the radio etc. On Saturday, the 4th, I heard a part of Hitler's speech from Koenigsberg. The front of a hotel at the railway station, illuminated, a torchlight procession in front of it, torch-bearers and swastika flag-bearers on the balconies and loudspeakers, I understood only occasional words. But the tone! The unctuous bawling, truly bawling, of a priest …

The Horst Wessel Song [Horst Wessel was a Nazi and petty criminal who became martyred by the Nazi Party after being killed in a dispute with a pimp. A song he had written earlier took his name and became the 'Party Anthem' and after Hitler's victory in 1933 the second National Anthem] between the announcements. An indignant denial, no harm will come to loyal Jews. Directly afterwards the Central Association of Jewish Citizens in Thuringia is banned because it had criticized the government in 'Talmudic fashion' and disparaged it.

Since then day after day commissioners appointed, provincial government trampled underfoot, flags raised, buildings taken over, people shot, newspapers banned, etc, etc. Yesterday, the dramaturg Karl Wolff [of the Dresden Schauspielhaus Theatre] dismissed 'by order of the Nazi Party' – not even in the name of the government – today the whole Saxon cabinet etc. etc. A complete revolution and party dictatorship. And all opposing forces as if vanished from the face of the earth

[…]

How long will I keep my post?

On top of the political pressure and misery of the constant pain in my left arm, the constant thinking about death. And the distressing and always unsuccessful efforts to obtain building money. And the hours of lighting stoves, washing up, keeping house. And the constant sitting at home. And not being able to work, to think.

FRIDAY, 31 MARCH 1933 – VICTOR KLEMPERER

Klemperer continues to observe growing Nazi oppression.

DRESDEN, GERMANY

Ever more hopeless. The boycott begins tomorrow. Yellow placards, men on guard.
Pressure to pay Christian employees two months salary, to dismiss Jewish ones. No
reply to the impressive letter of the Jews to the President of the Reich and to the
government.

[…]

No one dares make a move. The Dresden student body made a declaration today:
united behind … and the honour of German students forbids them to come into
contact with Jews. They are not allowed to enter the Student House. How much
Jewish money went towards this Student House only a few years ago!

In Munich Jewish University teachers have already been prevented from setting
foot in the University.

The proclamation and injunction of the boycott committee decrees 'Religion is
immaterial', only race matters. If, in the case of the owners of a business, the
husband is Jewish, the wife Christian or the other way round, then the business
counts as Jewish.

SATURDAY, 2 SEPTEMBER 1933 – FEY VON HASSELL

*Fey von Hassell lived in Rome while her father, Ulrich von Hassell, acted as German
Ambassador to Italy between 1932 and 1938. His appointment was made prior to
Hitler taking power in January, 1933.*

ROME, ITALY

My father has returned from Berlin, where he met Hitler.

He says that conversation with him is impossible. He never stops talking and
always on whatever subject happens to interest him at that moment. Any kind of
discussion is out of the question. However, if one is lucky enough to get a word in,
Hitler often agrees, which means that the last person to come in is right. All this
makes my father think that Hitler is a weak man.

My father managed to talk about the possibility of creating Italo-German
collaboration concerning the Balkans and said that Mussolini was interested in the
idea. Apparently, Hitler did not react. It was as though he simply had not heard; nor
for that matter did von Neurath [the German foreign minister].

Since Hitler abolished all other political parties last July, my father thinks that
democracy is over in Germany.

[…]

Membership of the Nazi
party rose from 800,000,
when Hitler came to power,
to over eight million by the
end of the war (one-fifth of the
German population).

ABOVE: Hitler amuses guests as they take afternoon tea at his Berghof mountain retreat.

AROUND WEDNESDAY, 10 JANUARY 1934 – ERNST THAELMANN

Thaelmann was arrested as leader of the German Communist Party, the KPD, on 3 March 1933. He wrote a record of the interrogation he underwent at the Gestapo prison in Berlin. He was detained without trial until his murder at Buchenwald on 18 August 1944.

BERLIN, GERMANY

It is nearly impossible to relate what happened for four and a half hours, from 5.00pm to 9.30pm in that interrogation room. Every conceivable cruel method of blackmail was used against me to obtain by force and at all costs confessions and statements both about comrades who had been arrested, and about political activities.

It began initially with that friendly 'good guy' approach as I had known some of these fellows when they were still members of Severing's Political Police [during the Weimar Republic]. Thus, they reasoned with me, etc., in order to learn, during that playfully conducted talk, something about this or that comrade and other matters that interested them. But the approach proved unsuccessful.

I was then brutally assaulted and in the process had four teeth knocked out of my jaw. This proved unsuccessful too. By way of a 'third act' they tried hypnosis which was likewise totally ineffective …

But the actual high point of this drama was the final act. They ordered me to take off my pants and then two men grabbed me by the back of the neck and placed me across a footstool. A uniformed Gestapo officer with a whip of hippopotamus hide in his hand then beat my buttocks with measured strokes, Driven wild with pain I repeatedly screamed at the top of my voice.

Then they held my mouth shut for a while and hit me in the face, and with a whip across chest and back. I then collapsed, rolled on the floor, always keeping face down and no longer replied to any of their questions. I received a few kicks yet here and there, covered my face, but was already so exhausted and my heart so strained, it nearly took my breath away.

And then there was that terrible thirst.

BELOW: A Nazi Party Rally held to mark the anniversary of the failed 1923 Munich Putsch, 9 November 1938. These celebrations concluded in Kristallnacht, 'Night of Broken Glass'.

LEFT: On the same day Hitler chats with Goering whilst other 'old fighters' in SA uniform look on. Behind Hitler to the right is Alfred Rosenberg, the Nazi Party philosopher.

24

Friday, 18 January 1935 – Police Captain
in Berlin

On 19 November 1934 Erna Haebich of the Botnang district of Stuttgart wrote to the Führer to enquire about the fate of her son who had been arrested. She received the following reply from the office of the Chief of Political Police of the Member States.

Berlin, Germany

To: Frau Erna Haebich

Stuttgart-Botnang, Neue Stuttgarter Str 48, I

In response to your enquiry sent to the Führer on 19th November 1934 I inform you on behalf of the office Political Police Commander of the Member States, Reichsführer, SS, Himmler that your son, Walter Haebich, was shot by firing squad on 1st July, 1934 in connection with the Roehm revolt.

As his execution took place in defence of the state, no further explanation is required.

Heil Hitler

(Signed), Captain of Police.

Sunday, 15 September 1935

At a special session of the German Parliament, called the Reich Party Rally of Freedom in Nuremberg, a law was 'passed' for the protection of German racial purity.

'Law for the Protection of German Blood and German Honour'

Imbued with the realization that the purity of German blood is a prerequisite for the continued existence of the German people, and inspired by the inflexible will to protect the German Nation for all times to come, the Reichstag has unanimously passed the following law which is hereby promulgated:

§1 (1) Marriages between Jews and subjects of German or related [*artverwandt*] blood are forbidden. Marriages concluded in spite of it are null and void, even if concluded abroad to circumvent this law.

[…]

§2 Extra-marital sexual intercourse between Jews and subjects of German or related blood is forbidden.

§3 Jews may not employ in their households female subjects of German or related blood under 45 years of age.

§4 (1) Jews are forbidden to fly the national flag of the Reich or display the national colours.

LEFT: Eva Braun was Hitler's mistress for 13 years until she became his wife for one day before their joint suicide in the Berlin bunker in 1945. This was taken before the outbreak of war.

(2) They may, however, show the Jewish colours. The right to do so is protected by the State.

§5 (1) Anybody violating the injunction listed in §1 will be punished by detention in a penitentiary.

(2) Any male violating the injunction listed in §2 will be punished by either a prison term or a penitentiary term.

(3) Anybody violating any of the provisions listed in either §3 or §4 will be punished by imprisonment for up to one year and a fine, or by either of these penalties.

[…]

The Führer and Reich Chancellor, Adolf Hitler

Reich Minister of the Interior, Frick

Reich Minister of Justice, Dr Guertner

Deputy Führer, R Hess

TUESDAY, 17 SEPTEMBER 1935 – VICTOR KLEMPERER

Klemperer comments below on the 'Nuremberg Laws' passed at the Reich Party Rally of Freedom.

DRESDEN, GERMANY

While I was writing yesterday, the Reichstag [meeting] in Nuremberg had already passed the laws on German blood and German honour (known as the Nuremberg

Adolf Hitler was an Austrian, born in 1889 in Braunau-am-Inn, the son of a customs official. He could so easily have been called Schickelgrüber. His father, who was illegitimate, went by that name for the first 39 years of his life before adopting the name of his presumed father, Johann Georg Hiedler (Hitler) in 1876, 13 years before Hitler was born. Adolf Hitler was an academic failure and survived by doing odd-jobs until the outbreak of the First World War. His only acknowledged talent was modest skill as an amateur artist.

Hitler served throughout the First World War as a corporal in a Bavarian regiment of the German army. He was wounded and gassed and won the Iron Cross.

Laws). Prison for marriages and extra-marital intercourse between Jews and 'Germans', prohibition on 'German' maids under 45 years of age, permission to show the 'Jewish flag', withdrawal of civil rights. And with what justification and what threats! Disgust makes one ill.

FRIDAY, 22 OCTOBER 1937 – LYUBOV VASILIEVNA SHAPORINA

Following the adoption of Stalin's Constitution the first elections to the Supreme Soviet were called in 1937. Lyubov Shaporina was the founder of the Leningrad Puppet Theatre and wife of the Soviet composer Yuri Shaporin. As members of the pre-revolutionary intelligentsia many of their friends and contemporaries were victims of Stalin's purges of the 1930s.

LENINGRAD, USSR

On the morning of the 22nd I woke up about three and couldn't go back to sleep till after 5. There were no trams, it was completely quiet outside, except for an occasional car passing by. Suddenly, I heard a burst of gunfire. And then another, ten minutes later. The shooting continued in bursts every ten, fifteen or twenty minutes until just after five. Then the trams started running, the street resumed its usual morning noise.

I opened the window and listened, trying to figure out where the shots were coming from. What could it mean? These were not the usual noises from the factory.

It was definitely gunfire. But where? The Peter and Paul Fortress is nearby. That was the only place they could be shooting. Were people being executed?

After all, between 3 to 5 in the morning it couldn't be a drill. Who were they shooting? And why?

This is what they call an election campaign. And our consciousness is so deadened that sensations just slide across its hard, glossy surface, leaving no impression. To spend all night hearing living people, and undoubtedly innocent people, being shot to death and not to lose your mind. And afterwards, just to fall asleep, to go on sleeping as though nothing had happened. How terrible.

[…]

In Detskoe Irina came home from school and said, 'They told us there are mass arrests going on right now. We need to rid ourselves of undesirable elements before the election!'

BELOW: A page from a 1936 anti-Semitic German publication 'Trau Keinem Fuchs auf Gruener Heid und Keinem Jud bei Seinem Eid, Ein Bilder Buch fuer Gross und Klein' by Elvira Bauer. The signpost reads 'Jews not wanted here'.

27

FRIDAY, 11 MARCH 1938 – CHANCELLOR KURT VON SCHUSCHNIGG

As Hitler's troops marched into Austria in the event known as the Anschluss Austrian Federal Chancellor Kurt von Schuschnigg was forced to make this radio broadcast before being placed under house arrest. He survived the war in a Nazi concentration camp and after liberation became a Professor of Political Science at St Louis University. In 1956 he became a naturalized US citizen.

VIENNA, AUSTRIA

This day has placed us in a tragic and decisive situation. I have to give my Austrian fellow countrymen the details of the events of today.

The German Government today handed to President Miklas an ultimatum, with a time limit, ordering him to nominate as chancellor a person designated by the German Government and to appoint members of a cabinet on the orders of the German Government; otherwise German troops would invade Austria.

I declare before the world that the reports launched in Germany concerning disorders by the workers, the shedding of streams of blood, and the creation of a situation beyond the control of the Austrian Government are lies from A to Z. President Miklas has asked me to tell the people of Austria that we have yielded to force since we are not prepared even in this terrible situation to shed blood. We have decided to order the troops to offer no resistance.

So I take leave of the Austrian people with the German word of farewell uttered from the depth of my heart: God protect Austria.

LATE AUGUST 1938 – EDWIN GREENING

Edwin Greening was an observer with the International Brigade, British Battalion. The letter below was written to the brother of Tom Howell, a volunteer with the International Brigade. Tom Howell was killed in action on 25 August 1938 at 2.30 in the afternoon. When General Franco obtained a complete and unconditional victory on 1 April 1939 the 'civil war' had claimed between 300,000 and 400,000 lives.

NEAR GANDESA, SPAIN

My Dear Dai Mark,

I regret having to write this, but Tom Howell was killed a few days ago (at 2.30pm, August 25th to be exact). We were together in an advanced position with the boys on some mountains called Sierra de Pandols, which overlook the town of Gandesa. I was … only 5 yards … from where Tom was posted.

[…]

From early morning things had been very quiet on our sector. Then suddenly the enemy sent over some trench mortars; one of the shells made a direct hit on a

Joseph Stalin was born in 1879 in Georgia, the son of a shoemaker. His real name was Joseph Vissarionovich Djugashvilli. He was training for the priesthood when he was expelled for his Marxist beliefs. He joined Lenin's Bolsheviks in 1903 and succeeded him as Soviet leader in 1927.

RIGHT: Adolf Hitler during his address at a cornerstone-laying ceremony to mark the start of construction of the Volkswagen factory at Fallersleben, June 1938. In the foreground is the prototype Volkswagen.

ABOVE: Hitler at the inauguration of a new Autobahn. By 1938 he had achieved 25% of his goal of building 7,300 miles of four-lane super highways criss-crossing Germany.

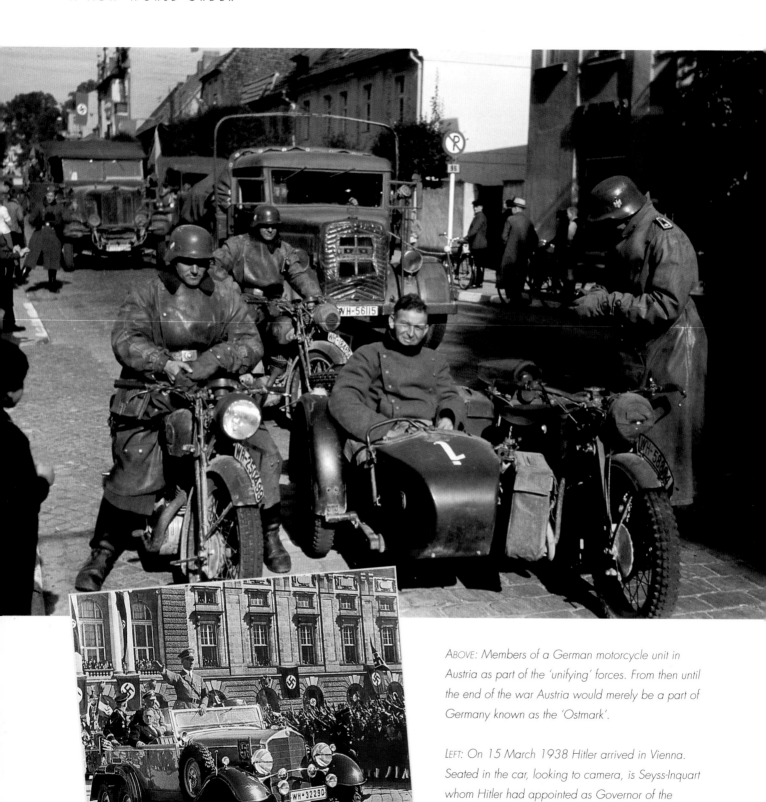

ABOVE: *Members of a German motorcycle unit in Austria as part of the 'unifying' forces. From then until the end of the war Austria would merely be a part of Germany known as the 'Ostmark'.*

LEFT: *On 15 March 1938 Hitler arrived in Vienna. Seated in the car, looking to camera, is Seyss-Inquart whom Hitler had appointed as Governor of the Ostmark.*

machine-gun post, nearly killing three men, a Spaniard and two Englishmen. I shouted to Tommy 'All right there Tom?' and he shouted back 'OK Edwin'.

Then this trench mortar landed near us. I called out again and receiving no answer, crawled to Tom's post, where I found him very badly wounded about the neck, chest and head. He was already unconscious and was passing away. I ran for the first aid man and we were there in two minutes, but Tom was, from the moment he was hit, beyond human aid … in two or three minutes, with his head resting on my knee, Tom passed away without regaining consciousness.
[…]
That night Alun Williams of Rhondda, a son of Huw Menai, and Lance Rogers of Merthyr, one of Tom's pals, carried his corpse to the little valley below, where he was to rest forever.

And there on that great mountain range, in a little grove of almond trees, we laid Tom Howell to rest. I said a few words of farewell but Tom is not alone there, all around lie the graves of many Spanish and English boys.
[…]
His thoughts were to the last always of his mother and the people at home. He lived and died a good fellow.

If fifty years pass I shall not forget.

SUNDAY, 11 SEPTEMBER 1938 – JOAN WILDISH

Following the loss of the family fortune in 1935 Joan began helping her parents run a guest house in SE London. In March 1938 she became engaged to a vicar. Her diary is deposited at the Imperial War Museum in London.

A year ago today. You pushed that barrow up the drive and shocked the whole household! I did not dream then that you would be the man I will marry.

The news is pretty bad. The world is on the brink of a huge cavity. It looks like WAR. We are all like ostriches hiding our heads in the sands. Oh! God don't let it happen. A Million, Million hearts must be lifted in that prayer. God don't let our men go, don't take our love. It is the women who must wait and worry.

You were so sweet. You tried to calm my fears. I share it with every other woman. The fear of saying 'Good-bye'.

MONDAY, 12 SEPTEMBER 1938 – MOYRA CHARLTON

Moyra Charlton was a young novelist. Later she was to drive an ambulance for the British Army at the nearby Colchester barracks. The extract is taken from her diary deposited at the Imperial War Museum, London.

BELOW: British Prime Minister Neville Chamberlain waves to cheering Germans as he drives to meet with Hitler in Munich, 29 September 1938. At the conference the fate of Czechoslovakia was determined. When he returned to England Chamberlain made the famous statement 'Peace in our time'.

TAKELEY, NEAR CHELMSFORD, ENGLAND

When we got in Hitler's speech was in progress [on the radio] and the Cowells [were] listening in. By missing some supper I managed to hear most of it, although I only understood a word here and there. The Führer was arresting and theatrical, making the most of an emotional delivery. From what I could gather in fragments from the Cowells, he means no surrender. Sooner or later he will have Czechoslovakia; his armament and defences will be ready before the autumn is out.

In each pause a crowd of thousands cheered and roared and howled. Hearing Hitler's very words and those frenzied howls brought home without doubt the terrible significance of it. Hitler means war. His people are as mad as he is, drunk with their brutal lust for gain.

How can one man plunge Europe into war? Thousands, millions of young lives to be spilt – and this is only twenty years after the last time? It can't be, God can't let it happen. But to hear those cheers made me awfully afraid.

At the end they sang 'Deutschland uber Alles' with swelling grandeur and poor Mrs Cowell ran out in tears. What can it be like for her, with relations and all her friends in Germany?

Benito Mussolini was born in Romanga in 1883, the son of a blacksmith. He was initially a member of the socialist movement, but was expelled for promoting Italian involvement in the First World War. He founded the Fascist Movement, became Prime Minister of Italy in 1922 and *Il Duce* (the leader) in 1925.

SATURDAY, 17 SEPTEMBER 1938 – HANNAH SENESH

The diary extract below was written at the age of 17. After the death of her father when she was six years old she grew up with her mother and older brother, George, in Budapest. Strongly committed to Zionism, she fled to Palestine in 1939. When she parachuted back into Hungary to rescue fellow Jews, she was taken prisoner. After months of torture she was executed in Budapest, which was by then under German control, in November 1944.

BUDAPEST, HUNGARY

We're living through indescribably tense days. The question is: Will there be war? The mobilization going on in various countries doesn't fill one with a great deal of confidence. No recent news concerning the discussions of Hitler and Chamberlain. The entire world is united in fearful suspense. I, for one, feel a numbing indifference because of all this waiting. The situation changes from minute to minute. Even the *idea* there may be war is abominable enough.

From my point of view, I'm glad George is in France, though Mother is extremely worried about him. Of course this is understandable. The devil take the Sudeten Germans and all the other Germans, along with their Führer. One feels better saying these things. Why is it necessary to ruin the world, turn it topsy-turvy, when everything could be so pleasant? Or is that impossible? Is it contrary to the nature of man?

TUESDAY, 27 SEPTEMBER 1938 – NEVILLE CHAMBERLAIN

LONDON, ENGLAND, BBC RADIO BROADCAST

How horrible, fantastic, incredible it is that we would be digging trenches and trying on gas-masks here because of a quarrel in a far-away country between people of whom we know nothing!

WEDNESDAY, 9 NOVEMBER 1938 – GESTAPO II MUELLER

Below is a secret telex message sent from the Secret State Police Headquarters in Berlin to all Regional and Local State Police Commands. It advises of the forthcoming attacks on Jews and synagogues. That night would become known as Kristallnacht or the 'Night of Broken Glass'. It was ordered by SD Head Heydrich as a reprisal for the murder in Paris of German diplomat Ernst vom Rath.

BERLIN, GERMANY BERLIN, NO 234 404 9TH NOVEMBER, 1938

TO: ALL REGIONAL AND LOCAL COMMANDS OF THE STATE POLICE

ATTENTION: CHIEFS OR DEPUTIES

This telex must be delivered at once in the fastest possible manner.

1 Operations against Jews, in particular against their synagogues will commence very soon throughout Germany. There must be no interference. However, arrangements should be made, in consultation with the General Police, to prevent looting and other excesses. [In all 101 synagogues were burnt down and 76 others demolished as well as 7,500 Jewish owned stores.]

2 Any vital archival material that might be in the synagogues must be secured by the fastest possible means.

3 Preparations must be made for the arrest of from 20,000 to 30,000 Jews within the Reich. In particular, affluent Jews are to be selected. Further directives will be forthcoming during the course of the night.

4 Should Jews be found in the possession of weapons during the impending operations the most severe measures must be taken. SS Verfuegungstruppen [predecessor of the Waffen-SS] and general SS may be called in for the overall operations. The State Police must under all circumstances maintain control of the operations by taking appropriate measures.

ADDENDUM FOR THE COLOGNE STATE POLICE:

The Cologne synagogue contains particularly important material. This must be secured at once in the fastest possible manner and in consultation with the Security Service.

GESTAPO II MUELLER

THIS TELEX IS CLASSIFIED 'SECRET'.

The Nazi definition of Jewishness was defined by the Nuremberg Laws of 1935. It included anyone with at least one Jewish grandparent, even when, in some cases, they had been practising Christians for generations.

SUNDAY, 27 NOVEMBER 1938 – VICTOR KLEMPERER

Klemperer was reported to the police for being in possession of concealed weapons. Here he recounts his experience of a house search and his arrest for questioning.

DRESDEN, GERMANY

On the morning of the 11th two policemen [arrived] accompanied by a 'resident of Doelzschen'. Did I have any weapons? – Certainly my sabre, perhaps even my bayonet as a war memento, but I wouldn't know where. – We have to help you find it. – The house was searched for hours. At the beginning Eva made the mistake of quite innocently telling one of the policemen he should not go through the clean linen cupboard without washing his hands. The man, considerably affronted, could hardly be calmed down. A second younger policeman was more friendly, the civilian was the worst. Pigsty etc. We said we had been without domestic help for months, many things were dusty and still unpacked. They rummaged through everything, chests and wooden constructions Eva had made were broken open with an axe. The sabre was found in a suitcase in the attic, the bayonet was not found. Among the books they found a copy of the Sozialistic Monatshefte [a Socialist monthly magazine – an SPD theoretical journal] [...] this was also confiscated. At one point when Eva wanted to fetch one of her tools, the young policeman ran after her; the older one called out: You are making us suspicious, you are making your situation worse. At about one o'clock the civilian and the older policeman left the house, the young one remained and took a statement. He was good-natured and courteous, I had the feeling he himself found the thing embarrassing.

[...]

You must dress and come to the court buildings at Muenchner Platz with me. There's nothing to fear, you will probably (!) be back by evening. I asked whether I was now under arrest. His reply was good-natured and noncommittal, it was only a war memento after all, I would probably be released right away. I was allowed to shave (with the door half open), I slipped Eva some money, and we made our way down to the tramcar. I was allowed to walk through the park alone while the policeman wheeled his bicycle at a distance behind me. We got on to the platform of the number 16, and got off at Muenchner Platz; the policeman kindly covered up the fact that I was being taken into custody. A wing in the court building: Public Prosecutor. A room with clerks and policemen. Sit down. The policeman had to copy the statement. He took me to a room with a typewriter. He led me back to the first room. I sat there apathetically. The policeman said: Perhaps you'll even be home in time for afternoon coffee. A clerk said: The Public Prosecutors' Office makes the decision. The policeman disappeared, I continued to sit there apathetically. Then

ABOVE: Following Kristallnacht *on 9 November 1938, Jewish shopkeepers clear up glass from broken windows in Berlin's Potsdamer Strasse.*

someone called: Take the man to relieve himself, and someone took me to the lavatory. Then: To Room X. There: This is the new committals room! More waiting. After a while a young man with a Party badge appeared, evidently the examining magistrate. You are Professor Klemperer? You can go.

[...]

At four o'clock I was on the street again with the curious feeling, free – but for how long? Since then we have both been unceasingly tormented by the question, go or stay? To go too early, to stay too late? To go where we have nothing, to remain in this corruption?

We are constantly trying to shed all subjective feelings of disgust, of injured pride, of mood and only weigh up the concrete facts of the situation. In the end we shall literally be able to throw dice for pro and contra. Our first response to events was to think it absolutely necessary to leave and we started making preparations and enquiries.

WEDNESDAY, 23 AUGUST 1939

After the signing of the Non-aggression Treaty between Germany and the Soviet Union a secret protocol was added on the same day. This pre-determined the general areas of German and Soviet occupation in Poland and the Baltic States after Germany's invasion of Poland in the west and the Soviet Union's invasion in the east later in September.

MOSCOW, USSR

SECRET ADDITIONAL PROTOCOL

On the occasion of the signature of the Nonaggression Pact between the German Reich and the Union of Socialist Soviet Republics the undersigned plenipotentiaries of each of the two parties discussed in strictly confidential conversations the question of the boundary of their respective spheres of influence in Eastern Europe. These conversations led to the following conclusions:

Charles de Gaulle was born in 1890 in Lille and graduated from St Cyr in 1911 and became a career soldier. He was badly wounded in 1916 and taken prisoner. After the war his military strategy advocated the use of air power supported by highly mobile armour, the basis of *blitzkrieg*.

LEFT: Adolf Hitler salutes the German Condor Legion at their victory parade in Berlin on 6 June 1939. They had fought in support of General Franco's forces during the Spanish civil war and gained valuable experience of front line action.

1. In the event of a territorial and political rearrangement in the areas belonging to the Baltic States (Finland, Estonia, Latvia, Lithuania), the northern boundary of Lithuania shall represent the boundary of the spheres of influence of Germany and the U.S.S.R. In this connection the interests of Lithuania in the Vilna area is recognized by each party.

2. In event of a territorial and political rearrangement of the area belonging to the Polish state the spheres of influence of Germany and the U.S.S.R. shall be bounded approximately by the line of the rivers Narew, Vistula and San.

The question of whether the interests of both parties make desirable the maintenance of an independent Polish state and how such a state should be bounded can only be definitely determined in the course of further political developments.

In any event both Governments will resolve this question by means of a friendly agreement.

3. With regard to Southeastern Europe attention is called by the Soviet side to its interests in Bessarabia. The German side declares its complete political disinterestedness in these areas.

4. This protocol shall be treated by both parties as strictly secret.

MOSCOW, AUGUST 23, 1939

FOR THE GOVERNMENT OF THE GERMAN REICH, V. RIBBENTROP

WITH FULL POWER OF GOVERNMENT OF THE U.S.S.R., V. MOLOTOV

THURSDAY, 24 AUGUST 1939 – DAWID SIERAKOWIAK

Dawid was the son of a Jewish family in the Polish town of Lodz.

LODZ, POLAND

Mobilization! We don't know if this is the real thing or not, but nearly every recruit is reporting. Many of our neighbours have already gone ... There's not the least hint of defeatism.

SATURDAY, 26 AUGUST 1939 – DAWID SIERAKOWIAK

As a patriotic Pole Dawid volunteered to help defend Poland.

LODZ, POLAND

Today I read Mayor [Jan] Kwapinski's appeal for volunteers to dig anti-aircraft ditches. Having got my parents' permission, I signed up immediately at the police station, as did all my schoolmates, and tomorrow morning I go to work. There are tens of thousands of volunteers ... Old Jews, young women, Hassidic Jews, all citizens (except the Germans) are rushing to volunteer. The bloody Hun will not pass!

Winston Churchill was born at Blenheim Palace in 1874, the grandson of the seventh Duke of Marlborough. He fought at the Battle of Omdurman and was a war correspondent during the Boer War. He was a leading political figure before the First World War, but, after the disaster of the Dardenelles Campaign, he joined the army and went to the Front in France.

Churchill returned to the government in 1917 and became Lloyd George's Minister for Munitions. He later became Secretary of State for War. He was Chancellor of the Exchequer during the 1920s, but spent much of the 1930s in the political wilderness, from where he constantly warned of the looming threat of war.

THURSDAY, 31 AUGUST 1939 – WILLIAM L. SHIRER

Shirer arrived in Berlin in the summer of 1934. He worked as the Chief of Universal News Service's Berlin office and later became a CBS correspondent. As well as his formal reports he maintained a personal diary of events and the attitudes he encountered. He later wrote, among other works, The Rise and Fall of the Third Reich, *one of the most acclaimed accounts of the period.*

BERLIN, GERMANY

Everybody against the war. People talking openly.

How can a country go into a major war with a population so dead against it?

People also kicking about being kept in the dark.

A German said to me last night : 'We know nothing. Why don't they tell us what's up?'

Optimism in official circles melting away this morning, I thought.

[Pierre] Huss [a correspondent of INS], thinks Hitler may have one great card left, an agreement with Stalin to attack the Poles in the back.

I highly doubt it, but after the Russo-German Pact anything is possible.

Some think the Big Boy [Hitler] is trying to get off the limb now – but how?

FRIDAY, 1 SEPTEMBER 1939 – JANINE PHILLIPS

On her tenth birthday in May 1939 Janine began keeping a diary while living with her Roman Catholic family outside Warsaw. With the aid of an illicit radio she was able to chronicle the events of the war. In the first year she filled a 1,000-page notebook. Returning to Warsaw in 1940 she was later to assist in the Warsaw uprising by setting up a first-aid post. Arrested by the Nazis after the collapse of the uprising she was taken to Germany as a prisoner-of-war. Upon her liberation in 1945 at the age of 16 she went to London where she eventually married.

OUTSIDE WARSAW, POLAND

Hitler has invaded Poland. We heard the bad news on the wireless a few minutes after spotting two aeroplanes circling round each other. Just before breakfast about ten minutes to ten, I was returning from the privy when I heard aeroplanes in the sky. I thought it was manoeuvres. Then I heard some machine-guns and then everyone came out from the house to see what was happening. Grandpa said, 'My God! It's war!' and rushed indoors to switch on the wireless. The grave news came in a special announcement that German forces have crossed the Polish border and our soldiers are defending our country. Everybody was stunned. With ears glued to the loudspeaker we were trying to catch the fading words. The battery or accumulator, or both, were packing up. When we could no longer hear a whisper from the

ABOVE: Dr Robert Ley with his wife, Inge, and Reichsleiter Max Amman leave the 'Day of German Art' exhibit in Munich in July 1939. Ley was responsible for the German Labour Front. He committed suicide in October 1945. Amman was head of Nazi press and publications.

RIGHT: A guard of honour lining the route of Hitler's motorcade at the celebration in Munich.

wireless set, Grandpa turned the switch off and looked at our anguished faces. He knelt in front of the picture of Jesus Christ and started to pray aloud. We repeated after Grandpa, 'Our Father who art in heaven, hallowed be thy name ...'

Soon after tea, Uncle Tadeusz, my new Aunt Aniela and Papa arrived from Warsaw with some more bad news. Papa said that we were not going back to Warsaw because it was safer to stay here, in the village. He arranged for a wagon to bring our winter clothes and other belongings. I wondered what will happen to our school, but Mama said that when a country is fighting for its survival, there is no time for schooling. All evening Papa has been trying to get the wireless going but did not succeed. Tomorrow, he'll try to get to Warsaw and see what can be done about the set which is so vital to us just now. Please, dear God, let our brave soldiers beat the nasty Germans.

FRIDAY, 1 SEPTEMBER 1939 – DAWID SIERAKOWIAK

Having helped construct defences for Lodz, Dawid anxiously awaited the inevitable attack of the Luftwaffe.

LODZ, POLAND

The German army has crossed the Polish border in several places. Air raids on Polish towns such as Cracow, Czetochowa, Katowice, Grodno, etc., have begun. Things are boiling, around the world. We're waiting for France and England to join the war; maybe even the United States. Meanwhile, we're repelling German attacks quite well. We had three alerts today, during which enemy planes were kept from approaching our town. I shall go to bed half dressed.

FRIDAY, 1 SEPTEMBER 1939 – VICTOR KLEMPERER

Like many other Jews still remaining in Germany at that time Klemperer was still unsure about emigrating to an unknown future.

DRESDEN, GERMANY

On Friday morning, 1st September, the young butcher's lad came and told us: There had been a wireless announcement, we already held Danzig and the Corridor, the war with Poland was under way, England and France remained neutral, I said to Eva, then a morphine injection or something similar was the best thing for us, our life was over. But then we said to one another, *that* could not possibly be the way things were, the boy had often reported absurd things (he was a perfect example of the way in which people take in news reports).

A little later we heard Hitler's agitated voice, then the usual roaring, but could not make anything out. We said to ourselves, if the report were even only half true they

Roosevelt was involved in government during the First World War as Assistant Secretary of the Navy. He was passionate about the sea and naval tradition.

_____

FDR campaigned for the vice-presidency in 1920 (unsuccessfully), but in 1921 he was struck down by polio. He was left almost completely paralysed.

_____

FDR won the presidency in 1932 and met the Great Depression head-on with the 'New Deal'. Its successful interventionist policies won Roosevelt a landslide victory in 1936.

must be already putting out the flags. Then down in town the dispatch of the outbreak of war. I asked several people whether English neutrality had been already been declared. Only an intelligent salesgirl in a cigar shop on Chemnitzer Platz said: No – that would really be a joke! At the baker's, at Vogel's, they said, as good as declared, all over in a few days!

A young man in front of the newspaper display: The English are cowards, they won't do anything! And thus with variations the general mood. Vox populi (butter seller, newspaper man, bill collector of the gas company etc. etc.) In the afternoon [I] read the Führer's speech. It seemed to me altogether pessimistic as far as the external and the internal position was concerned. Also all the regulations pointed and still point to more than a mere punitive expedition against Poland. And now this is the third day like this, it feels as if it has been three years: the waiting, the despairing, hoping, weighing up, not knowing. The newspaper yesterday, Saturday, vague and in fact anticipating a general outbreak of war: England, the attacker – English mobilization, French mobilization, they will bleed to death! etc. etc. But still no declaration of war on their side. Is it coming or will they fail to resist and merely demonstrate weakness?

EARLY SEPTEMBER 1939 – NELLA LAST

Nella Last began a diary in 1939 and continued writing for nearly thirty years.

BARROW-IN-FURNESS, ENGLAND

BEDTIME: Well, we know the worst. Whether it was a kind of incredulous stubbornness or a faith in my old astrological friend who was right in the last crisis when he said 'No War', I *never* thought it would come. Looking back I think it was akin to a belief in a fairy's wand which was going to be waved.

I'm a self-reliant kind of person, but today I've longed for a close woman friend – for the first time in my life. When I heard Mr. Chamberlain's voice, so slow and solemn, I seemed to see Southsea Prom the July before the last crisis. The fleet came into Portsmouth from Weymouth and there were hundreds of extra ratings walking up and down. There was a sameness about them that was not due to their clothes alone, and it puzzled me. It was the look on their faces – a slightly brooding, faraway look. They all had it – even the jolly-looking boys – and felt I wanted to rush up and ask them what they could see that I could not. And now I know.

The wind got up and brought rain, but on the Walney shore men and boys worked filling sand-bags. I could tell by the dazed look on many faces that I had not been alone in my belief that 'something' would turn up to prevent war. The boys brought a friend in and insisted on me joining in a game, but I could not keep it up. I've tried deep breathing, relaxing, knitting and more aspirins than I can remember, but all I can see are those boys with their look of 'beyond'.

TWO

BLITZKRIEG

SEPTEMBER 1939–JUNE 1940

When war came, on the morning of 1 September 1939, it was as swift and decisive as the Great War had been slow and ponderous. *Blitzkrieg* tactics worked with frightening efficiency. Stukas, screeching from above, destroyed the Polish airforce, bombed civilians and created mayhem. The panzer battalions devoured the open countryside of Poland at a prodigious speed. The *élan* of Germany's troops was a heady cocktail, mixing the warrior spirit of a new Germany with the avenging force of a country previously wronged and humiliated. They had a will to win that would prove to be extremely difficult to defeat.

An even more ominous mentality followed in the wake of the *Wehrmacht*. The ss death squads began their hideous work on the first day of invasion. *Einsatzgruppen* (Special Task Forces) immediately began the systematic slaughter of Poles and the destruction of their nation. One in six Poles would die in the war, many of them Jews. This was to be a war like no other.

Stalin's Red Army delivered on his Faustian pact with the Nazis and invaded eastern Poland two weeks later. The Soviets soon applied their own brand of ideological terror. The Poles were simultaneously at the mercy of the twentieth century's two most brutal regimes.

Britain and France honoured their pledge to defend Poland's sovereignty, but knew they could do little to help. They declared war and dropped millions of leaflets over Germany. Britain did initiate a bombing raid on the German navy and French troops occupied a few kilometres of German territory in the Saarland, but these were token gestures. German U-boats began their campaign against merchant ships and even sank a passenger ship, the *Athenia*, bound for Montreal. One hundred and twelve passengers were killed, many of them Americans. However, Roosevelt knew the mood of the American people and although he steadfastly reiterated America's neutrality, he was able to persuade Congress to permit the shipment of arms to Britain.

Hitler's plans for the invasion of western Europe were set within a month. He initially hoped to invade as early as 12 November. But bad weather prevented the clear skies the *Luftwaffe* required for the destruction of the French air force. Although there were extensive naval encounters and numerous bombing raids, 1940 brought what the British called a 'phoney war'. But it was merely a period of massive preparation. In the frozen north, there was nothing 'phoney' about the war between the Finns and the Soviets. Stalin had hoped to add Helsinki to his Red Empire. But Finnish resistance was far greater than he had imagined it would be and, after 14 weeks of fighting, a ceasefire was declared. Finland retained its independence in exchange for the forfeit of significant territory on its borders with the Soviet Union.

From as early as February, France and Britain had planned to close Germany's access to Swedish iron ore by occupying Norwegian ports. But they hesitated. More significantly, Hitler learned of the plan through German intelligence. He immediately began planning the invasion of Denmark and Norway, which began on 9 April. Danish resistance was minimal; Norwegian resistance, with modest support from British and Polish troops and the French Foreign Legion, lasted three months.

The 'phoney war' came to a dramatic end. Winston Churchill became Prime Minister of a coalition British government on 10 May, the day Hitler made his daring attack on Western Europe. The pace of the war, and the massive territorial gains for the Reich, escalated at an astonishing rate. The Dutch army surrendered on 14

BELOW: German troops watch the effect of shelling and bombing on Warsaw, 17 September 1939.

May. Rumours of thousands of dead in the bombing of Rotterdam horrified civilians everywhere. The French called the 'phoney war' a *drôle de guerre* (funny war), but what followed was far from funny. French pride would soon be hurt to the extent that the French people today are still divided about the morality of decisions taken during the fall of France, about the extent of collaboration under occupation and about actions taken after liberation.

The massive French line of defence, known as the Maginot Line, performed well at first and its 400,000

ABOVE: French civilians look upon the devastating effects of Blitzkrieg as Hitler's war machine turns west. June 1940.

defenders refused to surrender. Unfortunately, the line didn't extend far enough to the north, in the belief that the rugged and heavily forested area of the Ardennes was impenetrable to German armour. Germany knew that this was the basis of the French defensive strategy and so chose to do exactly what the French thought to be impossible. But first, Germany made a subtle but devastating feint by attacking through Holland and northern Belgium and thus drew the attention of the British Expeditionary Force and the French army towards the old killing fields of Flanders. Then, in a daring military gamble, von Rundstedt's Army Group cut through the Ardennes unseen and unopposed. They swung north, and, within ten days, reached the Channel, isolating the best of the French and British forces on ground difficult to defend with their backs to the sea.

But then Hitler made the first of many crucial errors that would prove to be critical to the outcome of the war. Instead of pressing home his advantage against the beleaguered Allies, he ordered the attack to halt so that he could concentrate his divisions on the conquest of Paris. Hitler's order to halt the attack was intercepted by British intelligence and the chance to evacuate the trapped soldiers was seized.

Thousands of crucially important British and French troops were brought off the beaches of Dunkirk as the French and Belgians held the ring around the port. However, the Belgian army surrendered at the end of May, Paris fell on 14 June and several days later Hitler and the *Wehrmacht* strode triumphantly down the Champs-Elysées. Hitler stood before Napoleon's tomb, a moment he said was the greatest and finest of his life. Europe was on the brink of catastrophe.

Shrewdly, Hitler decided not to impose an unconditional surrender on the French. That would merely alienate the French colonies, effectively handing all their resources to the Allies under General de Gaulle's Free French Forces. Instead, he allowed Marshal Pétain, the hero of Verdun, to form a government, which moved to Vichy in July, in what the French called the 'free zone'; but not before Hitler enjoyed a particular moment of revenge. The Franco–German Armistice agreement was signed in the same clearing in the forest of Compiègne, and in the same railway carriage, used for the signing of the Armistice at the end of the First World War. Hitler had the carriage removed from the nearby museum which housed it. He sat in the same chair in which Marshal Foch sat when he subjected the Germans to what Hitler regarded as a great humiliation. Now it was his turn. German honour was restored. The hatred in his heart, sown in the trenches of World War One, should have been satisfied by this symbolic moment and by the humbling of Germany's greatest enemy. But, on the contrary, time would tell that there would be no limit to the depths of Hitler's hatred, nor to the extent of the vengeance wrought by him on Germany's First World War opponents. Hitler returned to Berlin in triumph, even more convinced of his destiny and posing a threat to civilization that was greater than the world had ever faced before, or since.

SEPTEMBER 1939–JUNE 1940

1939

Sep. 1 Germany invades Poland.

Sep. 3 Britain and France declare war on Germany, as do Australia and New Zealand.

Sep. 5 The United States declares its neutrality.

Sep. 17 The German army reaches Brest-Litovsk. The Soviet Red Army invades Poland from the east.

Sep. 21 The Fascist Iron Guard of Romania assassinates the Prime Minister, Armand Calinescu.

Sep. 27 Warsaw surrenders.

Sep. 28 The Polish army surrenders; the country is partitioned.

Oct. 10 The deportation of Polish Jews begins.

Nov. 30 The Soviet Union invades Finland.

1940

Mar. 12 The Russo–Finnish War ends when Finland agrees to major territorial concessions.

Apr. 9 Germany invades Norway and Denmark.

May 10 Winston Churchill becomes British Prime Minister after the resignation of Neville Chamberlain.

May 10 Germany invades Holland, Belgium and Luxembourg. The German army also outflanks the Maginot Line by attacking France through the Ardennes.

May 14 The Dutch army surrenders.

May 26 The evacuation of British and French troops from Dunkirk begins. Over 330,000 return to England.

May 28 The Belgian army surrenders.

June 9 The Fall of Norway.

June 10 Italy declares war on France and Britain.

June 14 The German army enters Paris.

June 15 The French government appeals to America for direct help. America is unable to oblige.

June 17 Charles de Gaulle flies to London.

June 22 Marshal Pétain concludes an armistice with Germany. An autonomous French government is later declared at Vichy.

June 23 Hitler makes a triumphant visit to Paris.

SUNDAY, 3 SEPTEMBER 1939 – FRANKLIN D. ROOSEVELT

The American President speaking to the nation on radio intimates that America's position may not always remain one of being 'seated on the fence'.

RADIO ADDRESS
WASHINGTON DC, USA

'This nation remains a neutral nation, but I cannot ask that every American remain neutral in thought as well … Even a neutral cannot be asked to close his mind or conscience.'

SUNDAY, 3 SEPTEMBER 1939 – WILLIAM L. SHIRER

CBS correspondent William Shirer was in Berlin when war was declared. Despite claims by German radio of widespread support for the 'defensive' action against Poland, not all the German people wanted another war.

BERLIN, GERMANY

I was standing in the Wilhelmplatz about noon when the loud speakers suddenly announced that England had declared herself at war with Germany. Some 250 people were standing in the sun. They listened attentively to the announcement. When it was finished there was not a murmur. They just stood as before. Stunned. The people cannot realize yet that Hitler has led them into a world war. No issue has been created for them yet, though as this day wears on, it is plain that 'Albion's perfidy' will become the issue as it did in 1914. In 'Mein Kampf' Hitler says the greatest mistake the Kaiser made was to fight England, and Germany must never repeat that mistake.

[…]

On the faces of the people astonishment, depression. Until today they have been going about their business pretty much as usual. There were food cards and soap cards and you couldn't get gasoline and at night it was difficult stumbling around in the black-out. But the war in the west has seemed a bit far away to them – two moonlit nights and not a single Polish plane over Berlin to bring destruction – and the papers saying that German troops have been advancing all along the line, that the Polish air force has been destroyed. Last night I heard Germans talking of the 'Polish thing' lasting but a few weeks, or months at the most. Few believed that Britain and France would move. Ribbentrop was sure they wouldn't and had told the Führer, who believed him. The British and French had been accommodating before. Another Munich, why not? Yesterday, when it seemed that London and Paris were hesitating, everyone, including those in the Wilhelmstrasse, was optimistic. Why not?

46

Blitzkrieg (lightning war) was based on rapidly advancing tanks defended and supported by air power and motorized infantry. Attacks would strike through static defensive lines, advance deep into enemy territory and encircle and cut off defenders.

WEDNESDAY, 6 SEPTEMBER 1939 – DAWID SIERAKOWIAK

Dawid describes the increasing repression of the occupying German forces and also of the ethnic Germans in Poland whose aid the Wehrmacht *have come to.*

LODZ, POLAND

Oh, God, what's going on here? Panic, departures en masse, defeatism. The city, abandoned by its institutions and by the police, awaits the imminent arrival of the German army in terror. What's happened? People are running nervously from place to place, anxiously carrying around their worn-out possessions. An aimless confusion. I was on duty till 1.00am. I go to wake Rysio Wojcikowski for his turn. He is quite pessimistic, and tells me that some kind of evacuation of the city is contemplated. He tell me that in his father's office everything is packed, and that they're getting ready to leave Lodz at any minute. I'm astonished. How? Where? I hear that the Germans are going to occupy Lodz any hour now. At home I meet our neighbour Mr Grabinski, who has just returned from the city. He tells me of the great panic and frenzy seizing people. Throngs are leaving their homes on a dangerous migration to an uncertain future. There is crying and lamenting in the streets.

[…]

People are constantly on the move. Groups of men are heading toward Brzeziny to report for duty, while at the same time reservists and recruits are running away. Following them are women carrying bundles on their backs, filled with clothes, bedding and food. Even small children are running. All the leaders have left, so, for fun, we acted like we were the leaders, playing that role till noon.

Meanwhile, the situation is becoming ever more tense. Everyone has a different story to tell. Someone said that 150 English airplanes are waiting in Sieradz, another that the Germans have already occupied Zdunska Wola and are heading towards Lodz. The news gets stranger and more fantastic all the time.

Aunt Estera came to us with her children, and the house is filled with crying. Abek and Jankus ran away to Brzezny. What is to be done? What can be accomplished? […]

I go to bed, expecting, for the first time, a good night's sleep. Unfortunately, there is no fear of air raids now. When you want to take over something, you don't destroy it. In the evening a column of Polish soldiers began arriving in town. They march quietly, in formation. It's hard to tell whether they're advancing or retreating. […]

TUESDAY, 12 SEPTEMBER 1939 – DAWID SIERAKOWIAK

LODZ, POLAND

Jews are being seized again, and beaten and robbed. The store where my father works was robbed as the local Germans freely indulge their whims. People speak

Blitzkrieg tactics also included parachute drops and subversion and propaganda campaigns designed to cause confusion and undermine morale.

about the way Jews are treated at work: some are treated decently, but others are sadistically abused. Some Jews were ordered to stop working, to remove their clothes and stand face to the wall, at which point they were told they'd be shot. Shots were fired in their direction, and though nobody was killed, this was repeated a few times.

FRIDAY, 15 SEPTEMBER 1939 – RICHARD BROWN

Richard Brown, an Ipswich draughtsman was in a reserved occupation and thus not conscripted into the British Armed Forces. He 'did his bit' by volunteering as an ARP warden.

IPSWICH, ENGLAND

[…] In the land fighting poor little Poland is sticking it manfully. She is continually falling back but is giving a good account of herself. Warsaw is nearly surrounded and it seems my estimate of three months before being swamped will be an overestimate. Now the news seems to suggest that Russia will hit Poland in the back. She is talking of Poland oppressing her minorities, and she is certainly mobilizing. If she starts in this little war what will be the end of it? Why are they chumming up with the Germans who have always called them scum of the earth? Am afraid it means no good to us and probably Russia is after the Baltic States and Poland, as before the last war. […]

By the way I have estimated this affair will last five to six years. What a hell of a time. Five times 365 days each of which might produce some sort of fruitfulness in the way of air raid or bad news. Anyway who cares?

SUNDAY, 17 SEPTEMBER 1939 – COUNT VON SCHULENBURG

The German Ambassador in Moscow reports to Berlin on Stalin's intention to invade eastern Poland.

MOSCOW, RUSSIA, TELEGRAM
VERY URGENT, SECRET
NO.372 OF SEPTEMBER 17
REFERENCE MY TELEGRAM NO. 371 OF SEPTEMBER 16.
Stalin received me at 2 o'clock at night in the presence of Molotov and Voroshilov and declared that the Red Army would cross the Soviet border this morning at 6 o'clock along the whole line from Polozk to Kamenetz-Podolsk.

In order to avoid incidents, Stalin urgently requested that we see to it that German planes as of today do not fly east of the Bialystok-Brest-Litovsk-Lemberg Line. Soviet planes would begin today to bomb the district east of Lemberg.

[…]
In future all military matters that come up are to be handled by Lieutenant General Köstring directly with Voroshilov.

SCHULENBURG

MONDAY, 18 SEPTEMBER 1939 – RICHARD BROWN

As well as keeping a watchful eye out for German bombers and parachutists as a member of the Local Defence Volunteers, later to be renamed the Home Guard, Richard Brown follows political developments with a keen eye.

IPSWICH, ENGLAND

Well, well. Yesterday Russia marched into Poland on the thinnest of excuses. She said it was to protect her White Russian nationals because the Polish government does not now exist. The Poles are still resisting the Germans and making a few successes but, poor devils, they are no match really, I wonder what it means. Russia says she will remain neutral but will take over the Poland she used to have and leave Danzig and the corridor to Germany. Will she come into the war more actively, I wonder? If so and she tackles the French frontier with Germany, and then Italy and Spain decide not to remain neutral any longer, we look like being up against it.

Even so things are not so hopeless by any means.

THURSDAY, 21 SEPTEMBER 1939 – REINHARD HEYDRICH

Express letter from Heydrich to commanders of Security Police Special Units in Occupied Poland ordering the creation of Jewish ghettos in cities by the forced removal of Jews from rural areas.

BERLIN, GERMANY

TO THE COMMANDERS OF ALL SPECIAL UNITS OF SECURITY POLICE

SUBJECT: JEWISH QUESTION IN OCCUPIED TERRITORY

I refer to the meeting that took place today in Berlin and want to point out once again that the overall measures planned (thus, the final objective) must be kept strictly secret.

Distinctions must be drawn between:

1. the final objective (which will require more extensive time periods), and
2. the phases towards fulfilment of the final objective (which will be carried out on a short-term basis).

It is obvious that the task ahead cannot be determined from here in every detail. The following instructions and guidelines will simultaneously serve the purpose of prompting the commanders of Special Units to do some practical thinking.

Hitler committed 60 divisions and 1,500 planes to the attack on Poland. In the following five years Poland lost over 5.5 million people, mostly civilians, the highest casualty rate in the war (16 per cent of the population).

50

ABOVE: In all occupied territories, and eventually even in Germany, Jews were obliged to wear an identifying star or arm band.

I. The first prerequisite for the final objective will be, for one, the concentration of Jews from the countryside into larger cities.

This must be carried out expeditiously …

Attention must be paid to the requirement that only such cities may be designated as areas of concentration which are either railway junctions or are at least situated on a railway line. One prevailing basic rule will be that Jewish congregations of less than 500 members will be dissolved and moved to the nearest city of concentration …

II. Jewish Council of Elders.

1. Each Jewish congregation must set up a Jewish Council of Elders … it will be fully responsible, in the truest sense of the word, for an exact and prompt execution of all past or future directives.

2. In case of sabotage of such directives, the councils will be advised that most severe measures will be taken.

3. Deadlines given to the Jews for departure into the cities.

4. An overall account of all Jewish foodstuffs [?] and wartime [German version garbled] as well as of all industrial branches and factories important for the Four Year Plan within their respective regions …

[...]

V. To accomplish the objectives outlined I expect the fullest commitment of all forces of Security Police and Security Service.

Commanders of Special Units in adjoining positions must establish contact with each other at once in order to make sure that all affected regions will be completely covered.

[…]

SUNDAY, 1 OCTOBER 1939 – REICHS PROPAGANDA MINISTRY
Army Telex instructing propaganda film crews on the material they should shoot in occupied Poland for propaganda purposes in Germany and international distribution

2.47PM, BERLIN, GERMANY

REICHS PROPAGANDA MINISTRY

To: AOK 3 for Propaganda Company 501

AOK 8 for Propaganda Company 649

AOK 10 for Propaganda Company 637

AOK 14 or Propaganda Company 621

Luftfl. 1 for Luftwaffe Propaganda Company 1

Luftwaffenkommando Koenigsberg for Luftwaffe Propaganda Force

The Junkers 87 dive-bomber ('Stukas') were central to *blitzkrieg* tactics.

Widespread use of stereotypes in propaganda posters was made by all countries in the war.

LEFT: A German view of British colonial abuse.

RIGHT: An American view of Nazi brutality.

52

ABOVE: Young and old were exposed to the power of Goebbels' Propaganda Ministry.

RIGHT: A German poster for occupied Ukraine demonising the Soviet Commisars and focusing on atrocities in Vinnitsa.

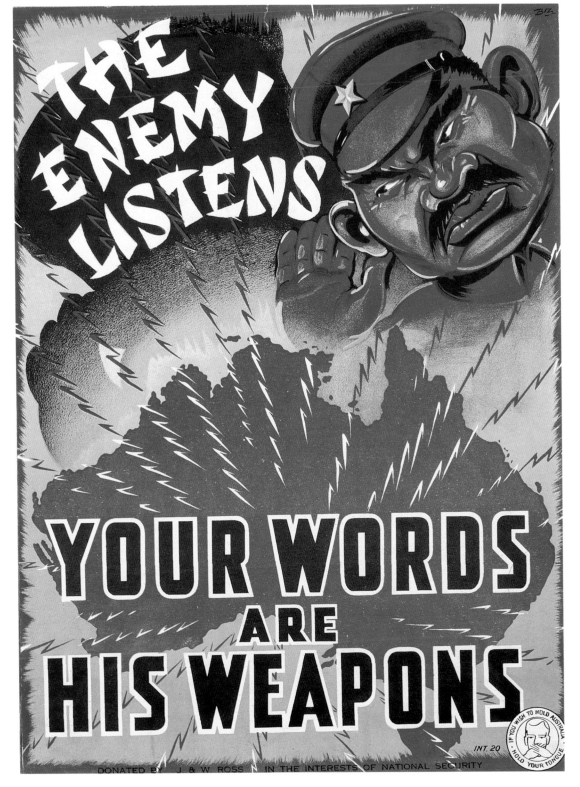

RIGHT: An official Australian warning on the proximity of Japan.

Propaganda Instructions of the Reichs Propaganda Ministry for 2nd October, 1939

1 In all reports Warsaw is not to be described as a town but as a Fortress.

2 Where possible shoot film on a larger scale than previously of Jewish types of all kinds from Warsaw and the whole surrounding area of occupation, not only whilst working [as forced labour] but also character studies. This [film] material should lead to a strengthening of anti-Semitic instruction in our domestic politics and in foreign affairs.

3 Report on the work at assembly points for our wounded and the work of our field hospitals

OKW/W Pr Id No. 2325/39 GEH.

OCTOBER 1939 – SERGEANT KARL FUCHS

A schoolteacher, Fuchs was conscripted into the Wehrmacht in October 1939.

GERMAN ARMY

LANGWASSER WEHRMACHT TRAINING CAMP, GERMANY

Dear Father

A week has gone by and we're now settled in at the military installation. The entire compound is superb! We have had our psychological examinations and, based upon these tests, I was assigned as a tank gunner. Now, of course, we have to learn and train until we perfect all of our skills. Infantry training is almost behind us and in eight weeks we have to be fit for combat. You, as an old soldier, know best what this means. The intensity of training is tremendous and there is no rest for anyone. All of us are eager to make progress and no one complains, least of all your son. You won't ever have to be ashamed of me; you can depend on me.

Several days ago I had to report to the captain of our company and speak to him about my plans for officer training. Today for the first time we had to practise shooting – five shots and five bull's-eyes for me! Next week we have training in shooting with rifles and machine guns. The recruits are looking forward to this training. All of us tank gunners need to be crack shots.

Next week we'll be able to climb into our tanks for the first time. Operating the vehicle will have to become second nature to us. Tanks are really awesome!

For the time being we will have no leave, at least not until New Year. Christmas will be spent in our barracks. I hope that all is well at home. Please write to me if you are able to come and visit. One more request; please take care of Mädi so that she doesn't feel so alone.

That's all for today. Sieg Heil and on to old England!

Your loyal son, Karl

The German offensive in western Europe was codenamed 'Fall Gelb' (Operation Yellow). It involved over 140 divisions.

WEDNESDAY, 31 JANUARY 1940 – HEINRICH HIMMLER

Directive by the Reichsführer-SS Himmler regarding the treatment of German women who are found having relationships with prisoners of war, endorsing the shaving of heads by 'kangaroo courts' prior to deportation to concentration camps.

Most of the officer corps of the Polish army were captured by the Soviets. Stalin later (1940) ordered 15,000 of them to be shot. It became known as the 'Katyn Massacre', after the name of the forest near Smolensk where 4,400 officers were massacred and dumped in mass graves.

BERLIN, GERMANY

REICHSFÜHRER-SS AND THE CHIEF OF GERMAN POLICE IN THE REICH MINISTRY OF THE INTERIOR

SIV 1 No.86 VI/39 -176-7 – SDB. STGB [CRIMINAL CODE].

To: a) The Regional and Local Commands of the State Police

b) Commanders of Security Police and Security Services, for your information

[...]

SUBJECT: CONTACTS WITH PRISONERS OF WAR

I. German women and girls whose contacts with prisoners of war are of a nature which grossly offends the sound instincts of the people are to be taken into protective custody until further notice, and are to be committed to a concentration camp for at least one year. A gross offence of the sound instincts of the people would be any social intercourse (e.g. parties, dances), especially all sexual intercourse.

II. Should women and girls of a locality want to pillory the woman in question publicly, or want to shave off her hair prior to her transportation to a concentration camp, the police are not to intervene.

SIGNED: HIMMLER

WITNESSED: ADMINISTRATIVE SECRETARY

FRIDAY, 2 FEBRUARY 1940 – GENERAL VON BLASKOWITZ

Extract from a memorandum by the Commander of the Army Group East, Colonel-General Blaskowitz, to the Commander of the German army Commander in Chief, Colonel General von Brauchitsch, on the treatment of the Polish population. In May, Blaskowitz was removed from the command of Army Group East for his criticism of German behaviour in Poland.

OCCUPIED POLAND

1. The military-political situation.

... the massacre of dozens of thousands of Jews and Poles which is taking place now is a mistake; as the population is very numerous it will not be possible either to bury the idea of a Polish state or to exterminate the Jews by these means. On the contrary the method of extermination does great harm, complicates the problems and makes them more dangerous than they could be if the actions were well thought over and determined.

TUESDAY, 27 FEBRUARY 1940 – WILLIAM L. SHIRER

BERLIN, GERMANY

Marvin has been digging out some interesting side-lights on life in war-time Germany.

She visited one of the nine Nazi Brides' Schools where the wives or prospective wives of S.S. men are taught to be good Hausfrauen [housewives] and fruitful producers of cannon-fodder for the next war. They are also taught how to read Nazi Newspapers and listen to the radio. Marvin noticed only two books in the girls dormitories, *The Belief in the Nordic State* and *Men* …

… because of the shortage of soap, which curtails laundering, Marvin found that German clergymen had taken to wearing clerical collars made of paper. They cost eight cents, can be worn inside out the second day, and are then thrown away …

Though the quota of Germans allowed entrance into America annually of 27,000, Marvin found a waiting-list of 248,000 names at the American consulate. Ninety-eight per cent were Jews – or about half the Jewish population left in Germany.

SATURDAY, 27 APRIL 1940 – HEINRICH HIMMLER

Guidelines of the Reichsführer-SS and Chief of German Police pertaining to the deportation of gypsies.

BERLIN, GERMANY

REICHSFÜHRER-SS AND CHIEF OF GERMAN POLICE IN THE REICH MINISTRY OF THE INTERIOR TO V.B. NO. 95/40

Guidelines for resettling Gypsies (First Transport from the western and northwestern border zone)

I. Determination of persons affected

1. To be deported [abgeschoben]

a) All Gypsies and Gypsies of mixed blood who have been rounded up and registered in accordance with the express latter of October 17,1939 from the Reich Security Main Office.

b) Under no circumstances may the maximum of 2,500 be exceeded.

[…]

III. Treatment in the assembly camps.

1. To begin with, all Gypsies are to be registered alphabetically according to their separate local police district. All Gypsies above 14 years of age will have a serial number affixed to their left forearm in coloured ink.

[…]

ABOVE: *The rounding-up and deportation of gypsies as well as Jews was an integral part of the Nazis' plan to create a pure Germany. The train here is departing from Asperg, Germany.*

BELOW: *The first stage of the deportation process was the obligatory gathering outside homes. This was supervised by the SS and Police. The gypsies here are being deported from Asperg, Germany.*

Saturday, 11 May 1940 – Dirk Van der Heide

In January 1941, Stanley Preston Young, a pro-British interventionist American, decided American opinion required persuasion. An editor for a book publisher, he wrote a moving, albeit fictitious, account of the German invasion of the Netherlands. The book, My Sister and I, sold 56,000 copies. It is the only known fiction included in this anthology.

ROTTERDAM, HOLLAND

The worst air-raid of all has just come. About half the houses on our street are gone. One bomb landed on the lawn by our air-shelter and one side of the shelter is caved in but the Baron and others are repairing it now. Mevrouw Hartog broke down and cried during the air-raid and got everyone very nervous when she yelled. I think she almost went crazy.

Heintje Klaes was killed! He went outside to see the light from the big flares and incendiary bombs and didn't come back. He slipped out. Heintje was not afraid of anything but the bombs got him. The whole house rocked when the bombs came close. We put our fingers in our ears but it didn't help much. The fire wagons are working outside now and half the people in the air-shelter including Uncle Pieter have gone out. I went for a while and they were taking dead people out of the bombed houses. Uncle Pieter sent me back up to stay with Keetje.
[...]
Mother is going to be surprised when she sees it. The street was just repaired last year and was very smooth and nice.
[...]
Uncle Pieter came back, he didn't find Mother because she is dead. I can't believe it but Uncle Pieter wouldn't lie. We aren't to tell Keetje yet. The ambulances are still screaming. I can't sleep or write any more now or anything.

Late June 1940 – Sapper Jack Toomey

Sapper Jack Toomey had served with the 42nd Divisional Postal Unit in France in May 1940. He wrote this letter to his cousins two weeks after his return to England following the evacuation of the BEF from Dunkirk.

BRITISH EXPEDITIONARY FORCE
DARLINGTON, ENGLAND

Well, it started and after two days and nights of constant 'alert' and all clears, we drunk [sic] a bottle of rum and another of Cognac biscuit to get some sleep, the air raid siren was in a church tower opposite and about twenty feet from our window. We were determined to sleep somehow. I was still drunk when I woke next day. A

The evacuation of Allied troops at Dunkirk wasn't entirely disciplined. The French were prevented from leaving until the end and were even fired on by British troops. The orderly queues, seen in the famous photographs and newsreels, were often supervised by officers with revolvers drawn.

LEFT: 14 June 1940: A soldier lies fallen before the Maginot Line, France's line of defence, perceived impenetrable until Hitler's troops circumvented it.

ABOVE: German infantry and supplies continue to advance through the Lowlands.

day or so later we were in a Chateau farmhouse affair when a dog fight developed about a thousand feet above us. Messerschmitts, Hurricanes and Spitfires were having a hell of a time. I don't know who won. I was too busy dodging planes, bullets, and AA shrapnel.

[...]

At another place they flew up and down the street, machine gunning as they went, nice quiet clean fun. At another place, the last before we made the Dunkirk dash, the dive-bombers came over and bombed us in the afternoon. Never look a dive bomber in the face, Bill, 'cos if you do you can bet your sweet life things are going to hum so, but pray hard and run, run like hell for the nearest ditches and dive into them. I got used to diving in the end, could make a flat dive from the middle of the road or a power dive from a lorry in one motion. Well, after the bombers had gone and we took stock of the wreckage and found we were all alive, they came back and threw out leaflets for our use.

We could hear M[achine].G[un]. fire and thought it was quite a shoot up by Jerry planes but when tracer shells started coming through the roof of our lorry I knew I

ABOVE: A formation of Heinkel He 111 bombers on their way to London in 1940. These were the most commonly used aircraft for raids by the German Luftwaffe on London.

59

RIGHT: 14 June 1940: Crude oil tanks burning outside Paris. This was the day that Paris fell to the Germans.

LEFT: The ruins caused by Blitzkrieg at a crossroads in Calais, late May 1940.

was wrong. Two shells took a knapsack from the box next to my head and threw it out of the back looking like cotton waste another went past my ear so close I felt the wind of it. All the time M.G. bullets were smacking and rickshetting [sic] of the struts. I just sat and gave up all hope of coming out of that lorry alive. However I heard a noise of a tank chugging past the lorry and the shooting stopped for us. The bloke driving the tanks saw us in the lorry and calmly tossed a hand grenade under the tailboard! After it had gone off and we found we were still alive we came out of that lorry with our hands in the clouds. There are pleasanter ways of committing suicide

The heroic stories of civilian boats going to help the evacuation ('little ships') which gave rise to the 'Dunkirk Spirit' were real enough, but didn't include everyone. The Rye fishing fleet refused to go, as did several lifeboat crews.

ABOVE: Two German soldiers rest after the occupation of Paris on 14 June 1940.

than fighting five tanks, an armoured wireless car and a plane, with a rifle. Well, they took us prisoner and while we were looking after the wounded the French opened fire and we were between the two fires, so back into the ditch we went. The main body of prisoners were run off to a nearby village. We lay in the ditch in a thunderstorm for two hours and then went back to our own lines. So much for my 'escape', more of a case of getting left behind.

When all was clear and we were on the outskirts of Dunkirk we stopped on a long raised road with the canal on either side and nice big trees sheltering us from the air. We got out and looked up – there were about seventy bombers (German make, naturally, we hadn't seen one of our planes for three weeks!!!) knocking hell out of the docks or what was left of them. From there to the beaches and they were black with troops waiting to go aboard only there were no boats. They gave us a raid that afternoon and evening and the following day they gave us a raid that lasted from dawn till dusk, about 17 hours. The fellows laid down on open beaches with the bombs falling alongside us, lucky it was sand, it killed the effect of the bombs. At the end of the day there were about 8 fellows killed and injured out of about 100,000. [...]

When we were about an hours run of Dover and thought we were safe a bomber came down and slammed three bombs at us – missed us by six feet and put all the lights out downstairs. We got to Dover at 2 a.m. and climbed aboard a train, we were still scared to light cigarettes, a light on the beaches meant a hail of bombs, and we just drowsed, at Reading we got out and shambled to the road outside, it was about 8.00am and people just going to work stopped and stared, we must have looked a mob, none of us shaved or wash for a week, our uniform was ripped and torn, with blood and oil stain. I had no equipment bar a tin hat and gas mask, a revolver I picked up from somewhere stuck out of my map pocket. One or two old dears took one look at us and burst into tears. I don't blame them. I frightened myself when I looked into a mirror.

THURSDAY, 20 JUNE 1940 – SERGEANT KARL FUCHS

A former schoolteacher, Fuchs was selected for Officer Training and subsequently was not permitted to serve the Führer *and the Fatherland in the campaign in the West.*

GERMAN ARMY, LANGWASSER WEHRMACHT TRAINING
CAMP, GERMANY
Dear Father,
You could be proud of your only son if he had been part of Germany's most magnificent victories. [France was now defeated.] Several weeks ago I told you that it was finally our turn to go to the front, but now nothing came of it. On 10 June our march unit went to the front without us. Orders from headquarters: All officer candidates have to remain here!! This time we weren't disappointed but enraged! We ran from officer to officer and finally to the commander, explaining to them that we would renounce all claims to becoming officers if we only got to go. All of our attempts were in vain. While we told them that we wanted to volunteer right away for the paratroopers, they asked us: 'Gentlemen, aren't you proud of your tank unit?' Obviously, they were trying to call upon our loyalty. Apparently our division is in dire need of young officers, much more so than any other division. We have become pessimists and believe that we will never get to go to the front – not even to take revenge on England.

[...]

BELOW: Hitler surveys the Champs-Elysées, Paris, his latest conquered capital, in a dawn motorcade on 23 June 1940. Amongst those with him was Albert Speer, his architect.

RIGHT: After leaving, Hitler remarked to Speer, 'Wasn't Paris beautiful? But Berlin must be made more beautiful. [...] when we are finished Paris will only be a shadow'.

THREE

BARBAROSSA

JULY 1940–NOVEMBER 1941

At the fall of France, Britain was Germany's only declared enemy left unconquered and still fighting. Its island position, its military traditions and the inspiring words of its leader Winston Churchill, portrayed it as the great bastion of freedom. And so it was, but the 'great bastion' was more bluff and courage than reality.

Despite the heroics of Dunkirk, the British army was in disarray, the Channel, a narrow stretch of water, was difficult for the Royal Navy to defend, and the Royal Air Force had only 600 fighters available to protect the skies. But Hitler was cautious. He was both anxious about the Royal Navy and the RAF and convinced that the British – whom he always considered his 'natural' allies – would negotiate for peace; at least following a period of 'persuasion' by *Luftwaffe* bombing.

However, the invasion plans were made and the date set for 5 August, but only after air superiority had been achieved. Reichsmarschall Göring, Hitler's chosen successor and Commander-in-Chief of the *Luftwaffe,* was given his moment of glory, while Hitler turned his mind towards what he'd always considered his and Germany's true destiny – Soviet Russia.

Whether Hitler needed air superiority, or whether he ever seriously considered the invasion of Britain, will always be the subject of academic debate. However, after several weeks of sparring over the Channel, the great battle of the skies was joined in August 1940. German losses were immediately high as they faced better machines and better pilots than they'd faced before.

The RAF was winning the aerial dogfights, but the *Luftwaffe* was inflicting heavy losses to planes on the ground. Stories of duels to the death by brave young heroes, set against the blue skies and green fields of southern England, lionized by the stirring speeches of Churchill, passed immediately into legend.

Eventually, *Luftwaffe* losses became too great. They were losing more fighters than the RAF and, significantly, when their pilots parachuted to safety they landed on British territory and were captured. British pilots landed back on home soil and went straight back into action; sometimes even on the same day.

Göring now turned his attention to civilians. If he couldn't master the RAF, he would undermine the military and the government by humbling the British in their homes. Bombing raids on London began in earnest on 7 September 1940. They increased in frequency and spread to other cities throughout the following months. Two hundred bombers battered London and other cities every night for months. On some nights, twice the number attacked. They continued until the following May, when Hitler needed them for his attack on the Soviet Union, by which time they had killed over 40,000 civilians and injured many more.

But, far from cowing the British, they had the reverse effect. Britain's belief in itself as the defender of freedom grew, its courage galvanized resistance groups in Europe and its resolve generated huge sympathy in America. It was particularly helpful to a newly re-elected and invigorated American President. Roosevelt was to become as vital to America's war effort as Churchill was to Britain's. It also led to immediate and uninhibited retaliation against German cities and sowed the first seeds of doubt about the invincibility of the German war machine.

There were, however, no seeds of doubt in Hitler's mind. When he had the 'living space' of Russia, he would have victory. All else was irrelevant. Hitler made his invasion plans at the beginning of 1941 for an attack in May with the vigour of a man driven by what he saw as his calling, but what others saw as the increasing myopia of a megalomaniac. However, events elsewhere delayed him sufficiently to make a critical difference later in the year.

Benito Mussolini's marauding Italian forces were not meeting with the success achieved by the German panzers. On 11 January, Hitler ordered German troops to bolster his ally's faltering campaigns in Greece and North Africa. The British and Australians had taken Tobruk and Benghazi, and the Greeks had forced the invading Italians back into Albania. Hitler was forced into a new Mediterranean and Balkan war and chose to commit Erwin Rommel to the campaign in North Africa.

British troops were sent to lend significant support to the defence of Greece. When, in March 1941, Hitler was denied access through Yugoslavia for his attack on Greece and he had to fight his way in, he delayed the planned invasion of Soviet Russia from May to June. All the same, the conquest of Yugoslavia and Greece was as awesomely swift as German victories elsewhere. Athens became the eleventh European capital to fall under Nazi control. Rommel soon reversed the defeats of the Italians in North Africa. The Nazi juggernaut seemed to be moving again with unstoppable potency.

The invasion of Soviet Russia began on 22 June and proceeded with alarming speed. But it faced only two obstacles that Hitler chose to ignore: the enormous distances for supply and communications and the fact that midsummer may have been too late to be able to sub-

ABOVE: Ukrainians in Kharkov study a map of Greater Germany in 1942.

jugate European Russia by the autumn, when military advances would be much more difficult.

As Soviet territory was consumed by German armour the death squads followed in their wake, beginning a regime of terror that would last for three years and bring brutality and death to countless millions. Eventually, the machine-gunning by the execution squads became so routinely boring and exhausting for the perpetrators that they resorted to throwing their victims into their mass graves alive. In fact, the relentless tedium of shootings was one of the reasons why death by gas became the preferred method of the Final Solution when it emerged during 1941.

By the end of September the Germans had besieged Leningrad and were within striking distance of Moscow, but summer was over and the critical midsummer delay in the Balkans began to assert its influence; but not in Hitler's mind. Kiev fell on 19 September and 600,000 Soviet troops were taken prisoner. There would be further successes in the south by the end of the year, which would give Hitler the greatest European empire in

ABOVE: German conquest by 1942 had created a European empire that Hitler always intended would be his. It was his New World Order. But from its earliest date it proved to be impossible to defend.

history and place him on the brink of victory, but, by then, autumn had turned to winter. It would be one of the worst on record.

1940

July 9 Romania voluntarily becomes a German protectorate.

July 16 Prince Fumimaro Konoe becomes the Japanese Prime Minister and announces that Japan will establish a 'New Order in Asia'.

Aug. 9 The Battle of Britain begins.

Aug. 15 'Aldertag' (Eagle Day), the day of the *Luftwaffe's* main attack in the Battle of Britain.

Sep. 7 Night-time German raids on London begin, the start of the 'Blitz'.

Sep. 13 Italian forces invade Egypt from Libya.

Sep. 22 The Japanese army takes control of large parts of French Indo-china around Hanoi.

Sep. 27 The tripartite pact is signed, agreeing military and economic co-operation between Germany, Japan and Italy.

Oct. 12 Hitler postpones operation 'Seelöwe' (Sea-lion), the invasion of Britain.

Oct. 28 Mussolini invades Greece.

Nov. 5 Franklin Roosevelt is re-elected for a third term as American President.

Nov. 14 A massive bombing raid on Coventry kills over 500 people. Britain retaliates with a raid on Hamburg.

1941

Feb. 12 General Erwin Rommel arrives in Libya to take control of the North Africa campaign.

Mar. 11 Roosevelt's 'Lease-Lend' bill is signed, which allows massive economic assistance to America's allies.

Mar. 25 Yugoslavia joins the Axis powers by signing the Tripartite Pact. It now includes Bulgaria, Hungary, Romania, Germany, Italy and Japan.

Mar. 27 Yugoslav coup.

Apr. 6 Axis forces invade Yugoslavia. German troops invade Greece.

Apr. 27 Athens surrenders to the German army.

June 22 Germany launches Operation Barbarossa, the invasion of the Soviet Union.

July 16 The German army takes Smolensk.

Sep. 8 The German army reaches the outskirts of Leningrad.

Sep. 19 The fall of Kiev.

Oct. 15 The fall of Odessa.

Oct. 16 General Hideki Tojo succeeds Prince Fumimaro Konoe as Japanese Prime Minister.

Oct. 24 The fall of Kharkov.

Nov. 3 The fall of Kursk.

Nov. 16 The second German attack on Moscow begins.

FRIDAY, 19 JULY 1940 – ADOLF HITLER

Hitler makes his final appeal for peace to Britain in the knowledge that three days earlier he had signed 'Directive 16 – On Preparations for a Landing Operation against England code-named Sea-Lion'.

THE REICHSTAG (SITTING AT THE KROLL OPERA HOUSE), BERLIN, GERMANY
Mr Churchill ought perhaps, for once, to believe me when I prophesy that a great Empire will be destroyed which it was never my intention to destroy or even to harm.

MONDAY, 2 SEPTEMBER 1940 – COLIN PERRY

Colin Perry was an 18-year-old office boy living in London. As the intensity of the Blitz grew he became ever more critical of Germany's attacks on civilians.

LONDON, ENGLAND
There is nothing glamorous about this war. It is not a war. It's a mass butchery. In the olden days the civilian population was far removed from the scene of battle, they were respected by both sides. Now Germans think fit to rain down their loads of

RIGHT: Spitfire Mk II P7895, of No. 72 Squadron, flying from RAF Acklington with Lt. R Deacon Elliot at the controls, over the Channel coast, April 1941.

BELOW: A fighter-bomber of the German Luftwaffe flies over the English Channel, 1940.

RIGHT: ATS girls operate a height and range-finder in conjunction with a 4.5" anti-aircraft ack-ack battery, December 1942.

death on harmless, defenceless civilians. Thank God Churchill is firm enough to refrain from ordering a retaliation bombing upon the German civilians. I fear I shouldn't be.

I suppose one day the sirens will cease to wail – but I cannot imagine it. It was wonderful coming home in the tube tonight during the raid and reading the Standard's most uplifting leader. 'London' it was entitled. I looked at the people around me as I read it – yes, they would uphold, with their smiling faces, the future of mankind.

SATURDAY, 7 SEPTEMBER 1940 – NELLA LAST

As the Battle of Britain raged above England, newspapers and towns throughout England were filled with the reality of war.

BARROW-IN-FURNESS, ENGLAND

The dinner-time post brought a bidding to a funeral, and it was a bit of a shock. It was a boy Cliff played with at Greenodd, and as far as circumstances permitted they were always good friends. John's home was at Bradford, but he spent all his holidays with his grandfather who had retired to Greenodd. Boarding school holidays were long, and his grandfather was getting old, so John used to cycle the twelve miles to Barrow most days it was fine. He loved the country so much, and they brought him to lie in the quiet of the hillside churchyard. He was one of those 'pilots reported missing'. As I stood with the mist hiding all the views of the hills around and the sad-looking grey water slipping over the golden sands of Morecombe Bay, I felt misery and pity grip me and I could have keened like an Irish biddy at a wake. Old Mr. Dickinson and his two sons were there with crowds of elderly worn-looking relations, and yet it was bright-eyed John who was lying there. I felt I'd had enough sorrow for one day, but when I picked up the local 'Mail' it was to see portraits of two bright-faced boys I'd watched grow up from babies who were reported 'missing' – both air pilots.

FRIDAY, 18 OCTOBER 1940 – COLIN PERRY

When Colin's street in London was bombed, his parents' home was hit by the blast of the explosion.

LONDON, ENGLAND

Churchill promised us 'blood, sweat and toil' – how true he was. I have already sampled sweat and toil. Last night I sampled blood. Just gone 8 last evening, Dad, Miller, Judd and myself were sitting in the dining room, comfortable in front of a roaring fire.

[...]

Suddenly there was a roar like an express train, a hurtling, a tearing, all-powerful, overwhelming rush. Together we sprang to our feet. We got no further. The earth seemed to split into a thousand fragments. A wrenching jar I thought signified the splitting of our outside wall. The subsiding rush of materials took, it seemed, all off the back. We reached the hall. We all thought the bomb had fallen a few yards outside the back, in Scotia's scrapyard. I quickly but calmly donned my jacket, put my keys in my pocket and my wallet in my inside pocket. I did this groping in the dark as I saw at a glance that our blackout was no more.

BELOW: Luftwaffe Capt. Von Werra poses with his Knight's Cross in 1941. Von Werra was the only German POW to successfully escape from the British. He was killed in action in the winter of 1941.

RIGHT: The devastation caused by German air-raids is clearly shown here in Balham High Street, London. The photograph was taken in early August 1940.

[…]

Outside there was a stifling, forbidding atmosphere. I stumbled over two masses of debris, clattered over piles of glass. The moon shone wanly upon this uncanny nightmare. Women in the hall were dizzy. I rushed outside in the front. I saw at once all the windows of the flats had been blasted open or out.

[…]

I meanwhile pelted headlong under a barrage of bursting shells along the Upper Tooting Road, past shopkeepers resignedly clearing up their smashed up shop fronts, up Beechcroft and so into Fishponds Road, which as the crow flies lies not fifty yards at the back of us. It was a turmoil of rushing, calm, tin-hatted wardens. Two demolition squads and rescue parties roared up. I counted ten ambulances. I quickly entered into the centre of the crowd, a crowd only of nurses, wardens, firemen. And there, amidst the dark suburban street, standing on charred debris of every description […] I confronted war in its most brutal savagery, I beheld blood, wounded, dying. I stood transfixed. My stomach did not turn, but from afar, yet so intimately, I found my brain dull registering sights of gore; I found I stood by the side of a little boy, his head a cake of blood, his arms – I knew not where they were. A small, plump, efficient voluntary nurse put her arms round him. He cried, every so often, very sobbingly for his Mummy. His Mummy was not to be seen. Quietly the nurse fingered his wounds – in a concise, firm, business-like voice, as if she was talking to a Mothers' meeting, 'Take him away immediately. Hospital case,' and turned her attention to the next.

[…]

they were victims of Hitler's massacre. I swear that I'll revenge them, I swear I will! I will not be a member of a bomber crew – never! If I thought for one moment I was a cog in the bringing about such terrible tragedy, I would rather be shot. My job is clear. I will be a fighter pilot, and I will shoot mercilessly the bloody Hun from out of the skies. I will fire callously at their bombers' crews, I will know no pity. I will blast these murderers, assassins, devils of all that is evil from out of the skies. May God grant me strength. For I have experienced the horror of war, the blood which has to be paid. If they had been soldiers – different. But women, children, my breed – I will not rest until I have fulfilled my vow.

BELOW: WAAFs position a barrage balloon over London's bomb damaged Temple area.

ABOVE: Night fires rage in London during the Blitz.

EARLY NOVEMBER 1940 – ADOLF HITLER

As raids on London continued, Hitler's mind was not distracted from his intentions on his eastern flank. In conversation with his Foreign Minister, Joachim von Ribbentrop, he confided.

At the start of the Battle of Britain, Fighter Command of the RAF had 900 fighters available, 600 could be airborne at any one time. The *Luftwaffe* had similar numbers.

BERLIN, GERMANY

'You know, Ribbentrop, if I made an agreement with Russia today, I'd still break it tomorrow – I just can't help it.'

SATURDAY, 21 JUNE 1941 – JOACHIM VON RIBBENTROP

Von Ribbentrop telegraphed his Ambassador in Moscow asking him to deliver the following message to the Soviet Foreign Minister, Molotov.

GERMAN FOREIGN MINISTER, BERLIN, GERMANY

VERY URGENT, STATE SECRET, BY RADIO

For the Ambassador personally.

1) On receipt of this telegram, all of the cipher material still there is to be destroyed. The radio set is to be put out of commission.

2) Please inform Herr Molotov at once that you have an urgent communication to make him and would therefore like to call on him immediately.

Then please make the following declaration to him.

… the Government of the Reich declares, therefore, that the Soviet Government, contrary to the obligations it assumed,

1) had not only continued, but even intensified its attempts to undermine Germany and Europe;

2) has adopted a more and more anti-German foreign policy;

3) had concentrated all its forces in readiness at the German border. Thereby the Soviet Government has broken its treaties with Germany and is about to attack Germany from the rear, in its struggle for life. The Führer has therefore ordered the German Armed Forces to oppose this threat with all the means at their disposal. End of declaration.

Please do not enter into any discussion of this communication. It is encumbent upon the Government of Soviet Russia to safeguard the security of the Embassy personnel.

SUNDAY, 22 JUNE 1941 – HERMIONE RANFURLY

Hermione worked as a civilian typist in the Special Operations Executive office in Cairo. Among the large numbers of British and Allied prisoners taken as the Germans advanced in North Africa was her husband Dan [Lord Ranfurly].

CAIRO, EGYPT

Germany has attacked Russia. The general opinion here is that Russia will be beaten in a few months – that she is ill equipped and without military leaders. Bonner Fellers is the only person I have met who thinks the Russians will survive – he has been to

73

BELOW: A self-propelled gun of the German Wehrmacht *drives through Athens after its fall to German forces on 27 April 1941.*

74

BELOW: 1942: Hitler strolls in the grounds of his Ukrainian headquarters at Vinnitsa with Hermann Göring.

LEFT: Hitler stands at the window of a train, saluting the crowds which throng the route.

RIGHT: Martin Bormann (Hitler's Private Secretary), an unidentified officer, Julius Schaub (Hitler's ADC) and Erich Koch, Gauleiter of East Prussia, in conversation with the Führer.

Russia fairly recently and says the Germans have bitten off more than they can chew.

I received a letter today which cheered me very much. It was from an RASC Captain McClure in Alexandria:

I was listening in to Radio Vatican yesterday at about 19.40 hours. The announcer was calling out a list of Prisoners of War. He spoke in English with a Scottish accent and gave out the regimental numbers in Italian. I heard him send one message as follows: 'Lord Ranfurly sends his love to his wife Countess Ranfurly, the Continental Hotel, Cairo.'

ABOVE:German Werhrmacht *troops advance through a Serbian village in April 1941.*

SUNDAY, 22 JUNE 1941 – ELENA SKRIYABINA

Elena Skriyabina commented in her diary on the news of the German attack.

LENINGRAD, USSR

Molotov's speech sounded hesitatingly and hastily, as if he was out of breath. His encouraging appeal seemed quite inappropriate. Immediately I had the feeling as if a monster was approaching slowly, threateningly, frightening everybody to death. After the news I ran out to the street. Panic was spreading around the city. People hastily exchanged a couple of words, then rushed to the shops, buying anything they saw. They were running in the streets like mad. Many went to the savings banks to take out their deposits. This wave absorbed me too. I also tried to receive cash from my savings book. But I came too late. The bank was empty, payments had been stopped. The crowd around was shouting and complaining. The June day blazed, the heat was unbearable. Somebody fainted, others were cursing. The day passed in a tense and uneasy mood. Only in the evening everything became strangely quiet. It seemed that everybody has hidden somewhere, possessed by terror.

SUNDAY, 22 JUNE 1941 – DAWID RUBINOWICZ

After the German occupation of Poland Dawid was forced with his family into the ghetto.

BIELINY GHETTO, POLAND

It was still dark when Father woke us all up and told us to listen to that terrible din coming from the north-east. It was such a din the earth quaked. The whole day thundering could be heard. Towards evening Jews dropped in from Kielce and said Soviet Russia was at war with the Germans, and only then did it dawn on me why there'd been that din all day.

SUNDAY, 22 JUNE 1941 – JOHN COLVILLE

Seconded from the British Foreign Office, John Colville served as Private Secretary to Prime Minister, Winston Churchill. Hitler's invasion of Russia was welcome news in Chequers, where the Prime Minister was staying.

CHEQUERS, ENGLAND

Awoken by the telephone with the news that Germany had attacked Russia. I went a round of the bedrooms breaking the news and produced a smile of satisfaction on the faces of the P.M., Eden and Winant. Winant, however, suspects it may all be a put-up job between Hitler and Stalin (later the P.M. and Cripps laughed this to scorn). […]

The P.M.'s broadcast was not ready till twenty minutes before he was due to deliver it and it gave me great anxiety, but even more so Eden who wanted to vet the text and couldn't. But when it was made it impressed us all: it was dramatic and it gave a clear decision of policy-support for Russia.

[...]

The P.M.'s view was that Russia was now at war; innocent peasants were being slaughtered; and we should forget about Soviet systems or the Comintern and extend our hand to fellow human beings in distress. The argument was extremely vehement. I have never spent a more enjoyable evening.

Later, the night being warm, we all walked in the garden and I gossiped with Edward Bridges while the P.M. continued an onslaught, begun at dinner, on the people who had let us in for this most unnecessary of all wars. He was harsh about Chamberlain whom he called 'the narrowest, most ignorant, most ungenerous of men'.

> 15 September 1940 has been called the 'Battle of Britain Day'. A major force of *Luftwaffe* bombers and fighter escort was met by the 'Big Wing', over 60 Hurricanes and Spitfires from RAF Duxford. The *Luftwaffe* lost over 60 planes, making a total of 175 losses for the preceding seven days of engagements.

WEDNESDAY, 25 JUNE 1941 – SERGEANT KARL FUCHS

Frustrated at not being able to fight on the western front, Karl writes with joy to his wife and son following his participation in the launch of Operation Barbarossa, Hitler's codename for the invasion of the Soviet Union.

GERMAN ARMY, VILNIUS, LITHUANIA

My dearest wife, my dear little Horsti,

After three days of heavy fighting we were finally granted a well-deserved day of rest. Unfortunately there is some maintenance work that has to be done.

How are you, my two loved ones? Since I received your postcard several days ago, I haven't heard from you. I suppose it's because of the postal delivery which, because of the huge distances now, only comes to us every three or four days. I myself am fine and healthy and today I received my first war decoration from our commander, namely, the tank assault medal. I wear it proudly and hope you are proud of me.

Up to now, all of the troops have had to accomplish quite a bit. The same goes for our machines and tanks. But, nevertheless, we're going to show those Bolshevik bums who's around here! They fight like hired hands – not like soldiers, no matter if they are men, women or children on the front lines. They're all no better than a bunch of scoundrels. By now, half of Europe is mobilised. The entry of Spain and Hungary on our side against this Bolshevik archenemy of the world overjoyed us all. Yes, Europe stands under the leadership of our beloved Führer Adolph Hitler, and he'll reshape it for a better future. The entry of all these volunteer armies into this war will cause the war to be over soon.

The impression that the battles have left on me will be with me forever …

YOUR KARRI

RIGHT: Fresh German Infantry reinforcements advance deeper into the Soviet Union.

ABOVE: The thirst of a dusty summer on the Eastern Front is quenched by local wine. The rains of autumn would eventually turn the parched earth to a sea of mud.

LATE JUNE 1941 – MACHA ROLNIKAS

Macha Rolnikas, a 14-year-old Jewish girl, was anxious about her father's future as he was known to have helped the Soviets during their occupation.

VILNIUS, LITHUANIA

The Nazis have occupied the Town. People are crying and talking about the Nazis' hatred of the Jews and Communists. And we, we are both. And on top of it all, Papa has been working very actively for the Soviets.

The invaders have posted a decree saying that all Communists have to register. Those who know of any Communists or members of any leftist organisation have to inform to let the Gestapo or S.S. know at once. Mama is uneasy. She asked to go through all of Papa's things. There are files about his defence of Communism. If they are found, we will be shot.

[…]

A woman crawling on all fours. Her hair is all tangled, her clothes dirty because of dragging herself along the ground, her eyes wide open, her face grimacing. Her bulging belly is resting on the ground. Covered with sweat, she stops every few minutes and, like an animal, pricks up her ears: is danger awaiting her somewhere? She is losing her strength. With each passing moment she feels a bit weaker. A great pain seizes her, shooting pains into her breast. She knows that her last moments are approaching, she is going to give birth.

ABOVE: A German Panzer Type III of the 18th Panzer Division.

LEFT: Infantry of Army Group Center advance with Panzer support near Moscow, 2 October 1941.

RIGHT: Panzers break through the 'Stalin Line' at Schitomiv in the Ukraine.

All night long, rolled up like a ball, exhausted, full of pain, she felt the approaching delivery. She continues to advance on all fours. She flops down in the middle of the street very close to the entrance, crawls to the sidewalk so as not to get run over. She won't ever get up again. She turns over and over in pain, in a kind of convulsion, writhing like a snake. She startles and death comes and interrupts her anguish at the same moment as her little girl comes to this world of pain and shadow. She is found next to her and is taken into the ghetto and named Ghettala. Poor little girl.

[…]

Early July 1941 – Paul Joseph Goebbels

Goebbels, head of Hitler's propaganda machine, had been an NSDAP member since 1924. An earlier diary entry stated 'Adolf Hitler, I love you'. His faith in the Reich's ability is undiminished in this entry which was written shortly after the launch of Operation Barbarossa.

The Führer thinks that the action will take about 4 months; I think – even less. Bolshevism will collapse as a house of cards. We are facing an unprecedented victorious campaign. We should act.

[….]

Cooperation with Russia was in fact a stain on our reputation. Now it is going to be washed out. The very thing we were struggling against for our whole lives, will now be destroyed. I tell this to the Führer and he agrees with me completely.

Thursday, 3 July 1941 – Joseph Stalin

Throughout the Soviet Union volunteers began the construction of defences as the former ally resumed a more traditional role. As Hitler's Wehrmacht and Luftwaffe drove deeper into the Soviet Union Stalin ordered that a 'scorched earth' must be left behind the retreating Soviet population and army.

ADDRESS TO THE RUSSIAN PEOPLE

MOSCOW, RUSSIA

In the case of a forced retreat of the Red Army units, all rolling stock must be evacuated; to the enemy must not be left a single engine, a single railway carriage, not a single pound of grain nor a gallon of fuel … In occupied regions conditions must be made unbearable for the enemy and all his accomplices. They must be hounded and annihilated at every step and their measures frustrated.

Reliable estimates suggest that total losses for the period June to October 1940 were Fighter command 800 fighters, *Luftwaffe* 1,300 aircraft.

During the 'Blitz' of London and other British cities, 43,000 British civilians were killed, 140,000 injured. *Luftwaffe* losses were light as, initially, anti-aircraft fire was ineffective.

SATURDAY, 2 AUGUST 1941 – HANS HINGST, VILNO

The order of the Region Commander of Vilno Hans Hingst on the treatment of the Jewish population.

1. All the Jews of both sexes from the city of Vilno must wear a yellow Zion star for identification on the left side of the chest and on the back.

2. The Jewish population is forbidden to use sidewalks. They must walk along the right side of the road and walk one after another.

3. The Jewish population is forbidden to stay in the boulevards and all public parks. The Jewish population is also forbidden to use street benches for rest.

4. The Jewish population is forbidden to use any kind of public transport, such as taxis, cabs, buses, steamboats etc. The owners or holders of all means of transport facilities should put a poster saying "Jews not allowed" on their vehicles so that they are clearly visible.

5. Anyone violating this order should be punished in the strictest way.

6. This order is effective from today.

THE REGIONAL COMMISSAR OF THE CITY OF VILNO/
SIGNATURE/HINGST.

VILNO, 2 AUGUST 1941

MONDAY, 4 AUGUST 1941 – SURGEON NIKOLAI MIKHAILOVICH AMOSOFF

Amosoff was a surgeon with field hospital PPG-2266. Here he describes the chaos of the front line shortly after the German invasion of the Soviet Union.

SOVIET ARMY

5KMS FROM ROSLAVL, RUSSIA

We are retreating all along the front – if there is such a thing as a 'front'. The communiques stress the enemy's losses – millions. Then why are Germans still advancing with such apparent ease? Where do they get fresh troops?

During the last month we have seen many troop trains going to the front – young, eager men, well dressed (our supply services have done a tremendous job). But they say we have few tanks, few planes; so much was lost during the first weeks of the war. How could we have been caught so much by surprise? Had we no intelligence service? Someone must have blundered. Who? We can only guess.

BELOW: In the summer of 1941 Heinrich Himmler, head of the SS, visited Minsk in Byelorussia. Whilst attending mass-executions the accompanying photographer was instructed not to take photographs of those events.

83

Of course no one discusses such matters. Even those who dislike and dread Stalin have learned to trust him. Propaganda? Yes and No. He has succeeded in transforming the country, though often by savage methods. We have built mighty industries out of nothing. Our men are brave. They have always been brave. Suicidal Russian courage, some call it. But why are we retreating? Why don't we attack?

[…]

Our armies are still retreating, and we are anxious to get into action. Those weeks of doing nothing, of being shoved around from station to station, were most unpleasant.

[…]

My team is all here: Lina, Liza, Tamara, Zoya. Good girls, all of them, though slightly afraid of the approaching action. Who can blame them?

[…]

we have two political officers: Zvereff, the second in command, and Shishkin. Zvereff is responsible for overall political education, and Shishkin for the morale of every person in the unit. His duties resemble those of the old army's chaplains – with one difference. All political officers and Commissars fight in the first ranks; they say that Germans shoot all of them out of hand.

THURSDAY, 7 AUGUST 1941 – THEODOR MORELL

On 4 August Hitler visited the headquarters of Army Group Centre on the Eastern Front. He confided to General Guderian: 'Had I known they had so many tanks as that, I'd have thought twice before invading.' The diary of Hitler's personal physician, Theodor Morell, written on the back of that day's menu – fried eggs, turnip, green beans, potatoes, strawberries – records the stress from which his patient was suffering.

RASTENBURG, EAST PRUSSIA

At Führer's headquarters. Saw Führer at one-thirty p.m. in map room. Said he'd been sitting down when he suddenly felt dizzy, with attacks of nausea and retching. Of late he's been looking pretty bad all the time, and pale … This bunker atmosphere has been getting him down for five or six weeks now.

Then Junge [an SS orderly] suddenly telephoned for me to come immediately to the Führer.

I hurried over. Face deathly white.

'I feel very bad now,' he said, 'much worse than I was earlier. Just now I suddenly felt giddy. I don't know what it is. Up here,' he said, indicating his left temple. 'I feel so strange. Over the last few days it's kept bothering me up there.' (For about a

Stalin was asked to join the Tripartite Axis Pact as late as November 1940, but his demands were too great and negotiations ended.

ABOVE: *East of Kiev a seemingly never-ending column of German troops extends to the horizon.*

week.) 'But a short while ago I had a terrific row, I got immensely worked up and since that time I've been feeling pretty low. And my stomach's been upset for a while too.'

Pulse normal. Forehead above eyebrows tender. Tremor in extended hands. No local tenderness of abdomen. Intestinal gases. Tongue furred. Liver of harder consistency and somewhat enlarged.

Injected Vitamultin-Calcium and Glyconorm. Bent the needle on insertion. Gave him a Yatren pill and twenty drops of Dolantin.

Blood pressure 172–4 (as opposed to 136mm normal). Fetched Septoiod and injected 10cc. Applied cold compresses to temples and left of head, and hot poultices.

Reflexes of the pupils [to light] good, eye movements unimpaired. Diagnosis: vascular spasms with rush of blood to temples.

Says he can hear a constant buzzing in left ear. Says he's had this before. Professor Eicken did not find anything.

Eight p.m. to see the Führer.

MONDAY, 8 SEPTEMBER 1941 – WEHRMACHT SUPREME COMMAND

This directive meant that the earlier directive [of 16.06.1941], according POWs protection in accordance with the Geneva Convention, was withdrawn.

BERLIN, GERMANY

SECRET!

DIRECTIVE ON THE TREATMENT OF SOVIET POWs IN ALL POW CAMPS.

I. General provisions on the treatment of Soviet POWs. Bolshevism is a deadly enemy of National Socialist Germany. For the first time the German soldier is facing an enemy, who has not just received military training, but is indoctrinated in the spirit of Bolshevism. Struggle against National Socialism is in his flesh and blood. He wages this struggle using all means: sabotage, subversive propaganda, arson, murder. Therefore the Bolshevik soldier has lost the privilege to be treated as a genuine soldier according to the Geneva Convention. […]

1. The faintest manifestations of protest or disobedience should be met with ruthless reprisals.

2. Weapons should be used ruthlessly to suppress resistance.

3. The escaping POWs should be shot at without warning and with the determination to hit the target.

Operation Barbarossa was launched at three am on the morning of 22 June, 1941; 3.6 million men, 3,600 tanks and over 2,700 aircraft attacked from German positions. The Red Army of nearly three million men, at least 10,000 tanks and 8,000 aircraft was over-run and suffered heavy defeats.

FRIDAY, 26 SEPTEMBER 1941 – HEINZ AUERSWALD

The following report by the Commissioner of the Jewish Residential District in Warsaw, Heinz Auerswald, pertains to the death toll in the Warsaw ghetto from January until August 1941.

WARSAW, POLAND

The increase of food supply deliveries referred to could not prevent the growing number of deaths which are due to the generally worsening misery of the Jews ever since the outbreak of war. The following numbers convey an impressive illustration of the death toll:

January	1941	898
February	1941	1,023
March	1941	1,608
April	1941	2,061
May	1941	3,821
June	1941	4,290
July	1941	5,550
August	1941	5,560

BELOW: Jewish residents in the Lodz Ghetto were obliged to wear their Yellow Stars on the right breast. A Jew of the ghetto is carried to the graveyard for burial by those who are yet to die.

RIGHT: *In the occupied town of Pavlovsk, near Leningrad, civilians queue to register with the occupying German Military Government.*

Barbarossa (Redbeard) was named after the German Holy Roman Emperor Frederick I, whose drowning in 1190 led to the myth that he would rise again when called by his countrymen to lead them back to glory.

———

The 'Barbarossa Jurisdiction Decree' exempted German soldiers from prosecution for crimes against Soviet civilians. A vicious 'scorched earth' policy was adopted by both sides.

A second reason for the increasing mortality rate is the spread of typhus in the Jewish residential district. Despite rigorous efforts to fight the spread of typhus, the curve has steadily risen. Weekly reports on typhus cases have remained on a fairly even level since July. They vary between 320 and 450 new cases. The last monthly figure (August) of 1788 persons is only somewhat higher than in the previous month, with 1736 new cases.

SUNDAY, 28 SEPTEMBER 1941 – H.G.

Extracts from the letters of H.G., a trader from Bremen, serving as a reserve policeman of the reserve battalion 105, to his wife about the participation of his unit in actions against Soviet Partisans.

BREMEN, OCCUPIED RUSSIA

[…] Yesterday I took part in combat. We advanced 25 kilometres through the forest, setting fire to every house and barn. The dwellings are abandoned. We burned all buildings in the forest so that the partisans would not be able to spend nights anywhere. We were 'incendiaries' in the literal sense of the word. We did not meet any partisans, those dogs had disappeared. Last evening I was very tired after the 25 km march through the wood.

SEPTEMBER/OCTOBER 1941 – MAJOR SHABALIN

The following extracts are from the diary of the NKVD (KGB) Major Shabalin. Head of the NKVD Special Section attached to the 50th Army from 6 to 19 October 1941. He was killed on 20 October trying to escape from the encirclement. His diary was translated by the German military for analysis. The Russian original was lost. It was translated by Chief of Staff of the 2nd Panzer Army Lt-Colonel Friedrich von Liebenstein.

6.9.41: The army is not the same that we thought and imagined it to be at home. Great shortage of everything. The attacks of our armies are disappointing.

7.9.41: We interrogated a red haired German POW, a ragged fellow, covered with lice and extremely stupid. ...

10.9.41: The situation with the personnel is very bad, practically the whole army consists of men, whose homes have been captured by the Germans. They want to go home. The passivity at the front, immobility in the trenches demoralise the soldiers. There are some cases of drinking among the officers and political Commissars. Sometimes people do not come back from reconnaissance missions ...

14.10.41: The enemy has encircled us. Incessant gunfire. Cannon, mortar and sub-machinegun exchanges. Danger and fear all day long. And this is not to mention the swamp, the forest, and the problem of passing the night. I have not slept since the 12th, have not read a newspaper since 8 October.

15.10.41: Terrifying! I wander around, dead bodies, was horrors and permanent bombardment everywhere. I am hungry and had no sleep again. Took a bottle of alcohol. Went to the forest for reconnaissance. Our total destruction is obvious. The army is beaten, its supply train is destroyed. I am writing sitting in a forest by a bonfire. In the morning I lost all my Cheka (KGB) officers, and now I am alone among strangers. The army has disintegrated.

16.10.41: I spent the night in the forest. I had no bread for three days. There are a lot of soldiers in the forest, but no officers. Throughout the night and the morning the Germans were firing at the forest from all kind of weapons. At about 7 A.M. we got up and marched north. The gunfire continues. During a halt I managed to wash my face and hands. ...

19.10.41: All night long we were marching through the rain across marshlands. Pitch dark. I was wet to the bone, my right foot has swollen; very difficult to walk.

THURSDAY, 23 OCTOBER 1941 – REICH SECURITY MAIN OFFICE

Decree by the Reich Security Main Office, pertaining to the ban on further Jewish emigration from Belgium and France.

All the policies concerning Hitler's Jewish 'problem' culminated in the 'Final solution' in 1941, which would be systematic and total. There would be no witnesses, new death camps would be built, and gas chambers would be the preferred method of killing.

Berlin, Germany

IV B 4b (RZ) 2920/41g (984)

To the Authorised Representative of the Chief of Security Police and Security Service Belgium and France

Att. SS brigadier General Thomas, Brussels

Subject: Emigration of Jews Secret!

Reference: none

The Reichsführer-SS and the Chief of German Police has directed that the emigration of Jews is to be halted at once. (The evacuation operations remain unaffected by this decree.) I ask you to notify the appropriate German authorities within their administrative regions of this decree.

Only in individual cases of a very particular nature, for instance, if national interest might be positively affected, may the emigration of some individual Jews be granted as long as a ruling to this effect has been obtained beforehand from the Reich Security Main Office.

Acting as deputy signed: Müller

RIGHT: Objects confiscated in round-ups and from people about to be deported from the ghetto were sorted by those who remained behind for the future use of the Reich.

ABOVE: Jews provided their own police force, as here in Lodz, in many of the ghettos created during the German occupation of Poland.

RIGHT: The Lodz Ghetto ran a highly successful manufacturing operation. By working for the Master Race there was a small hope of survival.

FRIDAY, 24 OCTOBER 1941– CHIEF OF ORDER POLICE

Express letter by the Chief of Order Police (Ordnungspolizei), pertaining to the deportation of Jews from the 'Altreich' and the 'Protectorate of Bohemia and Moravia'.

BERLIN, GERMANY

1) During the period November 1 to December 4, 1941, the Security Police of the Altreich, the Ostmark [Austria] and the Protectorate of Bohemia and Moravia will ship 50,000 Jews to the east into the vicinities of Riga and Minsk. Resettlement will take place by means of railway transport *[Reichbahn]*, with each train carrying 1,000 persons. The transport will be assembled in Berlin, Hamburg, Hanover, Dortmund, Muenster, Duesseldorf, Cologne, Frankfurt/Main, Kassel, Stuttgart, Nuremberg, Munich, Vienna, Breslau, Prague, and Brünn.

[...]

SIGNED: DALUEGE.

THURSDAY, 13 NOVEMBER 1941 – MUNICIPAL POLICE CAPTAIN

Report by the Sector Command North, Litzmannstadt, pertaining to the arrival of transports of deported Jews.

LITZMANNSTADT, FORMERLY LODZ, POLAND

I. JEWS:

During the period of October 16,1941 until November 4, 1941 inclusively, 19,827 Jews were received from the Altreich at Radegast Station and sent to the ghetto. The Jews (primarily older women and men) arrived here daily during the period previously stated with 20 transports in special trains of the Reichbahn (passenger carriages), carrying on average 1,000 persons.

ARRIVALS WERE AS FOLLOWS:

5 transports from Vienna ....with	5,000 Jews
5 transports from Prague ....with	5,000 Jews
4 transports from Berlin ....with	4,187 Jews
2 transports from Cologne ....with	2,007 Jews
1 transport from Luxembourg .....with	512 Jews
1 transport from Frankfurt ....with	1,113 Jews
1 transport from Hamburg ....with	1,034 Jews
1 transport from Düsseldorf ....with	984 Jews
20 transports	**totalling 19,837 Jews**

[...]

[Signature illegible]

CAPTAIN OF MUNICIPAL POLICE AND DEPUTY SECTOR COMMANDER

Hitler intended to totally destroy Moscow and Leningrad if they fell. Lenin's coffin was removed from its Mausoleum in Red Square and the Soviet government left the Kremlin. However, Stalin stayed in Moscow. German panzer units got within 18 miles of the city in November 1941.

FRIDAY, 21 NOVEMBER 1941 – VOLODYA VOLKOV

From the diary of Volodya Volkov, 16 years old, from Leningrad written during the German siege.

LENINGRAD, USSR

21 November: Life as usual

22 November: Life as usual

23 November: Life is getting worse

24 November: Life as usual

25 November: Life is getting worse. Bread rations – 250 grams for workers, 125 grams for dependants

26 November: Daddy is feeling worse, Mummy and Aunt Pasha too

27 November: life is getting worse

[...]

16 December: Daddy is feeling worse, Mummy and Aunt Pasha are still on sick leave.

17 December: Life is getting worse

18 December: No news from Misha. Daddy is getting worse.

19 December: Daddy is getting worse. Mummy has swollen from hunger, aunt Pasha too.

20 December: Nina is getting weaker. Daddy is getting worse. Mummy is getting worse. I am still staggering around.

21 December: Life is getting worse

22 December: received six photos for daddy's passport

23 December: Daddy is worse. Mummy is worse. Aunt Pasha is worse.

24 December: Daddy is very weak, I missed many days /at school?/

25 December: Daddy dies at 10 A.M. Bread rations were increased. 350 grams for workers, 200 grams for dependants. We cannot receive our food rations. Mummy and Aunt Pasha have hunger swellings ...

THURSDAY, 1 JANUARY 1942 – KARL RUPP

Letter from German soldier Karl Rupp to his wife in Stuttgart from the Central Front.

My dear wife!

I am writing my first letter to you in the New Year. To your parcel you attached a letter with the words so nice, that I am reading it again and again. You are writing about yourself and about our Jurgen, and it reads like a greeting from a different world. You know, sometimes I think that I am not able to answer you properly in my letters. But the way from home to us is so long, and we have to put away all

ABOVE: The German troops were poorly equipped for the Russian winter as they approached the vicinity of Moscow in late 1941.

The siege of Leningrad lasted 900 days. It is estimated that almost a million people died in the atrocious conditions.

thoughts about Motherland and home. Even if I am trying to write a really nice letter, it will still be just a report about our limited little world, and there will hardly be a place for anything apart from our worries and hopes. And still every time when I am holding a greeting from you in my hands, there is a warm feeling in my soul, but everybody here has to suppress his feelings for the thousandth time, and even if somebody tries to express them in words, the result is pathetic. But if we will be able to get out of here, everything will be as it has been, and we will become closer to each other again…

MONDAY, 23 FEBRUARY 1942 – WILHELM PRÜLLER

Prüller, a fanatical Nazi, chronicled his service to the Fatherland. His dedication to the cause led him to include a letter he wrote to an unknown girl about her boyfriend Martin in his diary.

GERMAN ARMY, RUSSIA

A long time ago a letter to an unknown soldier of the Company arrived in which a girl asked to have information about her dead fiancé. No one wanted to answer it, because there's no one here any more who was there when he fell. Thus the letter wandered about from one to the other till it finally landed in my lap. I wrote her the following letter:

Dear Mitzi Trunka,

After various detours I received your letter to an unknown soldier of the Feldpost No. 13694; no one dared to answer it. And I can't really blame anyone, for none of the Kameraden who were near your fiancé when he met his hero's death is with the Company anymore. He fell on 4th August in the great battle of Uman, as the Company was attacking Ternovka, and lies buried with other Kameraden who fell there in Tishkova, 50km. north-east of Uman. A shot in the lung robbed him of his life at the very height of his power. The death was immediate and without pain.

Believe me Fräulein Trunka, that I understand only too well how much you miss your beloved fallen man. But you are a German girl; and as such you are as enthusiastic about our fight for the life or death of our people as all of us who are here on the front. Later in your life, in a quiet hour, when you have your own family, you will remember with thanks beyond measure all the victims which this gigantic battle has demanded, and will demand. It is they, and only they, who will have saved us and our children from a life of degradation and shame, of distress and desperation.

I know that it is easy to speak of the sacrifice which the relatives of those who fell must take upon themselves, when one does not have to bear the brunt oneself; but as

Germany had no less than 55 per cent of its army committed to the Eastern Front for the entire four-year duration of the campaign.

ABOVE: As the winter deepened and 1941 turned to 1942, supplies of winter clothing had still not reached the German soldiers in the deepening snow.

I think, so does each of us here. And every one of us is sure that the grain that is sown will one day be reaped.

Just as we here are proud to have taken part in this great fight, so you, Fräulein Trunka, must be proud to have made such a heavy sacrifice for this fight. It was not, it shall not be in vain!

Your Martin shall be avenged! The survival of our great Fatherland, our imperishable people, and the victory over our accursed enemies shall have been accomplished partly through his death.

In our remembrance of the fallen Kameraden left behind I include you too, Fräulein Trunka; and greet you in sincere sympathy.

Long Live the Führer!
Prüller

FRIDAY, 21 JUNE 1940 – MICHAEL SCOTT, RAF

Scott took off for his first operational flight on 24 January 1942. He was killed in action that night. His sister, Flora, added a footnote to his diary in her handwriting: 'First Operation Flight. Missing over North Sea. Never heard of again.' Among Michael Scott's effects was found a last letter, to be opened only in the event of his death.

ENGLAND

Dear Daddy,

As this will only be read after my death it may seem a somewhat macabre document, but I do not want you to look on it in that way. I have always had a feeling that our stay on earth, that thing we call 'Life', is but a transitory stage in our development and that the dreaded monosyllable 'Death' ought not to indicate anything to be feared. I have had my fling and must now pass on to the next stage, the consummation of all earthly experiences. So don't worry about me: I shall be alright.

[...]

You know I hated the idea of war, and that hate will remain with me forever. What has kept me going is the spiritual force to be derived from music, its reflection in my own feelings, and the power it has to uplift a soul above earthly things. Mark has the same experience as I have, though his medium of encouragement is poetry. Now I am off to the source of music and can fulfil the vague longing of my soul in the becoming part of the fountain whence all good comes. I have no belief in an omnipresent God, but I do believe most strongly in a spiritual force which was the source of our being, and which will be our ultimate good. If there is anything worth fighting for, it is the right to follow on our own paths to this good, and to prevent our children from having their souls sterilised by Nazi doctrines. The most terrible aspects of Nazism is its system of education, of driving in instead of leading out, and putting the state above all things spiritual. And so I have been fighting.

A few last words about the disposal of my scant possessions. I would like Mark to have my wireless and records in the belief that he will get out of them as much as I have done. I have nothing else in intrinsic value except my golf clubs, which you can distribute as you think fit. If I have any balance at the bank, which is extremely unlikely, could you arrange that Flora use it as she thinks fit, as she has been an ideal pair in our relationship to each other.

All I can do is to voice my faith that this war will end in victory and that you will have many years before you in which to resume a normal civil life. Good luck to you!

Combined military losses (Soviet 13.6 million, German 3 million) amounted to more than two-thirds of the total of all military casualties in the war.

———

Soviet civilian losses may have been as high as another 13 million, including 33,000 Jews murdered by machine gun by the SS in a single incident at the Babi Yar ravine near Kiev.

PART TWO

GLOBAL CONFLICT

FOUR

A DAY THAT WILL LIVE IN INFAMY

NOVEMBER 1941-SEPTEMBER 1942

Hitler didn't have long to savour the conquests of his massive empire in November 1941. Even he must have realized that with his mighty army stretched thinly along a line from Leningrad to the Crimea, and significantly short of their targets, the Russian winter would exact a terrible toll.

Moscow and Leningrad had held out long enough. Not even the *Wehrmacht*'s panzers could fight in temperatures as low as –30 degrees centigrade. No amount of German warrior spirit or fascist fanaticism could insulate the ordinary soldiers from the intolerable conditions. They froze to death in their improvised shelters; their self-confidence ebbed away day by day as winter's grip tightened. Hitler demanded attack after attack, he refused all compromise and turned a deaf ear to advice.

The Soviet army lived and trained with their winter. They knew its dangers, but were not afraid of it. At the beginning of December, the Red Army launched a surprise attack cloaked in a fearsome blizzard. Ninety Soviet divisions, fresh from bases in Siberia, where the unusually harsh conditions of Moscow were normal, threw themselves with patriotic fervour against the exhausted Germans. The German lines were breached and they were forced to give ground. Many months of killing, starvation and deadly cold were yet to come, but Moscow would not be added to Hitler's bloody collection of trophies.

In the midst of the drama of the Eastern Front, the war took a dramatic new turn at the beginning of December 1941. By then, Japan had been campaigning to create its Asian Empire for ten years, following the occupation of Manchuria in 1931. The war with China began in earnest in 1937. Inevitably, Japanese expansion in Asia threatened the European spheres of interest in the area, became a real geographical threat to Australia and, ultimately, brought it face to face with the United States.

Japan had few natural resources. Control of vital raw materials became both the goal of expansion and the means by which expansion could be achieved. By the middle of 1941, the Japanese armed forces were running out of fuel. The Americans had imposed an embargo in response to Japanese expansion on the Asian mainland. The two nations were on a collision path. But both the

BELOW: Fires rage into the night following the Japanese attack on the US fleet in Pearl Harbor, Honolulu.

RIGHT: Franklyn Delano Roosevelt, 32nd President of the United States, in an official Kodachrome portrait taken in 1944.

Americans, and the European powers with colonies in South East Asia, expected that Japan would strike in the south in pursuit of raw materials, especially the oil of the Dutch East Indies. This was indeed the ultimate direction of their expansion, but they had a devastating trump card to play first.

When over 350 Japanese planes attacked the American Pacific Fleet at Pearl Harbor on 7 December 1941, they inflicted huge losses on the ships at anchor and on the planes on their airfields. It was a daring and seemingly successful surprise attack. But it had the reverse of its intended effect and wasn't sufficiently well supported to be decisive. Instead of neutralizing America in the war, it galvanized it. They could have continued their attacks at Pearl Harbor practically unopposed and inflicted even more damage. They could have hunted down the American aircraft carriers (which, fortuitously, happened to be at sea). They could even have invaded Hawaii and denied the Americans any kind of foothold in the Pacific. But they chose to withdraw, content with their devastating, but indecisive attack. It would take three years to unfold, but the scenario from then on was simply a matter of time before America's massive military and economic potential stirred itself, until it became irresistible.

Significantly for the war in Europe, Hitler made another crucial and inexplicable decision after Roosevelt declared war on Japan. Convinced that the Japanese would defeat the Americans and that his panzers would eventually break through on the Eastern Front, and determined to share the spoils of Japan's victory in the Pacific, he declared war on America. It was another fatal mistake. All he succeeded in doing was to give Churchill the vital lifeline he needed. The full weight of America's resources was now committed to the Allied cause. Hitler had, in effect, signed his own death warrant.

Within months, Japan proceeded to accumulate a colossal empire in the Pacific. Thousands of islands and millions of people came under Japanese control. Their regime was also brutal, like their Axis partners and their enemy the Soviet Union, but theirs was driven, not by ideological hatred, but by a medieval warrior's contempt for a defeated and thus cowardly enemy. Notwithstanding the motives, their victims suffered as greatly as the victims in Europe: summary executions, beatings, starvation and torture. Thousands died, and a legacy was left which will live long in the memories of the nations involved.

In Europe, spring broke the deadly impasse on the Eastern Front. Hitler was still confident of success in Leningrad and Moscow and now concentrated his forces on a drive through the Caucasus. It was to be another mistake, perhaps the most significant of all.

The most disturbing feature of the war in western Europe in 1942 was the escalating death toll among civilians, as both Britain and Germany targeted cities in their war of aerial attrition. The *Luftwaffe* turned its attention to a much wider range of British targets, including cities like Bath, Exeter, Canterbury and York, in what became known as the Baedeker raids. The RAF responded with increasingly ferocious raids on German cities. The first '1,000 bomber' raid was flown over Cologne in May. Unprecedented damage was done.

In the Pacific, the inevitable naval showdown came in two crucial battles. The battle of the Coral Sea in May 1942 inflicted heavy losses on both sides, including the loss of the American carrier *Lexington*. But the outcome

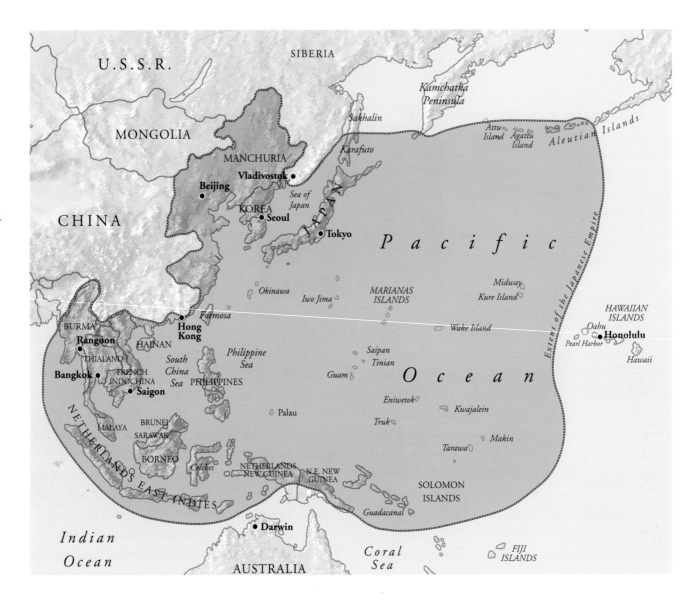

ABOVE: By the middle of 1942, Japan had conquered a huge empire in the Pacific, on the Asian mainland and in SE Asia.

marginally favoured the Americans, a situation that would be critical to a decisive battle in June.

The Japanese attack on Midway was a massive invasion force. Their mission was to capture the island as a staging post for the conquest of Hawaii. But the Americans deciphered the Japanese invasion code and knew they were coming. It was a colossal battle lasting for four days. American aircraft losses were crippling and, in the first four waves of attacks, had failed to hit their targets. But, on the morning of 5 June, the pendulum of the Pacific war swung in America's favour with the astonishing success of a fifth wave of attack. In a matter of minutes the US dive-bomber pilots caught the Japanese carriers crowded with planes re-fuelling. Three carriers were sunk and a fourth followed soon afterwards.

Admiral Yamamoto withdrew his task force. It was the first defeat ever inflicted on the Japanese navy.

NOVEMBER 1941–SEPTEMBER 1942

1941

Nov. 27 The Red Army counter-attacks on the Eastern Front. The Germans retreat from Rostov-on-Don, the first backward step for the *Wehrmacht*.

Dec. 6 The Soviets launch a massive counter-attack around Moscow. The Russian winter is at its worst.

Dec. 7 The Japanese attack Pearl Harbor.

Dec. 8 America declares war on Japan, as does Britain.

Dec. 11 Germany and Italy declare war on America.

1942

Jan. 5 A great Soviet offensive on all fronts commences.

Jan. 11 Japan captures Kuala Lumpur.

Feb 1. Vidkun Quisling, Norwegian fascist, becomes prime minister.

Feb. 14 Japanese troops advance to the Dutch East Indies.

Feb. 15 Singapore falls to Japan.

Feb. 19 The Japanese air force bombs Darwin, Australia.

Mar. 30 Japan advances through Burma.

Apr. 5 The Japanese air force bombs Colombo, Sri Lanka.

Apr. 9 The fall of the Bataan Peninsula in the Philippines and the beginning of the 'Death March'.

Apr. 14 Pierre Laval becomes Premier of Vichy France.

Apr. 18 The Germans mount a spring offensive in the Ukraine, aiming for the Caucasus oilfields.

Apr. 18 US bombers attack Tokyo, the 'Doolittle Raid'.

Apr. 23 German raids on historic places in Britain begin, the 'Baedeker' raids.

May 1 Mandalay falls to the Japanese.

May 4 The Battle of the Coral Sea, between the US and Japanese fleets, begins.

May 6 The surrender of Corregidor in the Philippines to the Japanese.

May 27 Reinhard Heydrich, the acting 'Protector' of Bohemia and Moravia, is shot by the Czechoslovak resistance. Two weeks later Hitler orders the village of Lidice to be destroyed and all males over 16 to be shot.

May 30 The first British 1,000 bomber raid on Germany is launched, against Cologne.

June 4 The Battle of Midway begins. The Japanese lose four aircraft carriers.

June 21 Rommel's Afrika Korps takes Tobruk.

July 7 Japanese forces take Guadalcanal in the Solomons.

July 21 Japanese forces land on New Guinea.

July 28 The German army takes Rostov and most of the northern Caucasus.

Aug. 19 The beginning of the Battle of Stalingrad.

SATURDAY, 1 FEBRUARY 1941 – MEMORANDUM FROM THE CHIEF OF NAVAL OPERATIONS

Despite intelligence gathering operations offering warnings to the US these warnings went unheeded.

WASHINGTON, DC USA

Op-16-F-2, (SC) A16-3/EF37

Serial No. 09716

FEB. 1, 1941

CONFIDENTIAL 10465

FROM: CHIEF OF NAVAL OPERATIONS

TO: COMMANDER-IN-CHIEF, PACIFIC FLEET

SUBJECT: RUMORED JAPANESE ATTACK ON PEARL HARBOR.

1. The following is forwarded for your information.

Under the date of 27 January the American Ambassador at Tokyo telegraphed the State Department to the following effect:

'The Peruvian Minister has informed a member of my staff that he has heard from many sources, including a Japanese source, that in the event of trouble breaking out between the United States and Japan, the Japanese intend to make a surprise attack against Pearl Harbor with all of their strength and employing all of their equipment. The Peruvian Minister considered the rumors fantastic. Nevertheless he considered them of sufficient importance to convey this information to a member of my staff.'

2. The Division of Naval Intelligences places no credence in these rumors. Furthermore, based on known data regarding the present disposition and employment of Japanese naval and army forces, no move against Pearl Harbor appears imminent or planned for in the foreseeable future.

JULES JAMES, By direction

Dictated Jan. 31, 1941 by Lieut. Comdr. A.H. McCollum

Typed by M.E. Morse.

CC – Com 14 10466 Confidential

(SC)A16-3 / EF37

The winter of 1941–42 was one of the worst on record in the Moscow area. The *Wehrmacht* had made no provision for a winter war. German losses were running at 5,000 a day.

In the first week of December the temperature dropped to −35 degrees centigrade in Moscow. German tanks wouldn't start; men froze to death in their thousands.

On 6 December, in the midst of a fierce blizzard, the Red Army attacked the German positions around Moscow using specially trained ski troops. The *Wehrmacht* fell back, losing 30,000 men.

TUESDAY, 5 AUGUST 1941 – 2ND LT JOHN LEWIS

*John, on active service as a Commando in the Western Desert, kept a journal for his
girlfriend Mirren in Oxford. He was instrumental in the restructuring of Commando
operations and was considered to be one of those responsible for the establishment
of the SAS. He was killed by fire from a German fighter after an operation in Libya on
30 December 1941.*

NO 8 COMMANDO, BRITISH ARMY

I have just got back from a patrol which was sprung on me unexpectedly last night
while I was writing to you. I have been up all night and it is now seven o'clock and
life is just beginning to stir in the reserve lines where we are. Sleepy figures are rising
out of the ground as though by magic and moving very slowly about their business.
Last night was the first patrol which I have led which did not achieve its object. We
went out to cut the telephone line to an enemy listening post and try to nab listeners.
When we were still a hundred yards short of the wire we ran slap into the middle of a
German minefield and set one mine off before we knew we were in it. The Germans
S Mine is an ugly affair: it consists of a metal box containing an explosive charge
surrounded by about 400 steel balls. The mine is buried in the ground and when set
off it jumps about four feet in the air before exploding, when it scatters its shrapnel in
all directions for about 100 yards just chest-high. We were incredibly lucky to get
away without a single casualty, but it took us so long to get out of the mine-field
without tripping another that we had to come back with nothing accomplished except
the fact of having located the minefield. This was disappointing, for I had discovered
the telephone line and listening post in the first place and was naturally keen to clean
it up, but now someone else will get the job, for we move to another line tonight. The
listening post is in an old disabled tank and must be incredibly useful to Jerry, for it is
only a few hundred yards from our most forward posts.

Damm this war! What do you want to know about S Mines and listening posts?
Nothing, less than nothing, you wish you'd never heard of them, I'm sure, and so do
I when I realise to whom this nonsense is dedicated. And yet I suppose it is as well
for you to get used to my bad habit of complete preoccupation with whatever
enterprise I have a hand in at any time, at any rate if you are considering
encouraging this correspondence.

This is a paltry letter, just nibbling and picking at the icing of the cake without
getting down either to the plums or the more humdrum stuff that holds them together.
But I'll send it off as it is and hope that a new start will inspire something more
worthy of your consideration.

Au revoir, my true love…

JOHN

SATURDAY, 22 NOVEMBER 1941 – WESLEY JOHN HEIDT

Wes Heidt, Fireman 1st Class, US Navy, stationed with his brother Bud on the USS *Arizona, finally writes a letter to his mother from Pearl Harbor.*

PEARL HARBOR, HAWAII

Hello Mum,

This is your bad son again. Boy Have I been catching hell for not writing. I don't know why you worry about us so much, if anything happened to us you would hear from the navy the first thing; so until you hear from them there is no need of worrying. I am safer on this battleboat than I would be driving back and forth to work if I was home. You know mum there is lots of times I start to write but I have to give up because there is nothing to writeabout except our activities and I am not aloud [sic] to say anything about them. Tell Louise not to repeat anything her sailor friends say. for instance she wrote and said that some sailor told her that he saw our ship in Honolulu, and mentioned his name. Now if that letter to us happened to be censored the navy could find who her sailor friend was and have him court-martialled for giving out information. So please be careful and don't believe anything you hear. The only time to expect us home is when you see us. I don't think it will be long now. I hope. Well woppie I must say goodbye for now and will write soon.

Your third and favourite Son…

SUNDAY, 7 DECEMBER 1941 – MAJ. GEN. EMERY S. ADAMS, US ARMY

Draft of telegram from Maj. Gen. Emery S. Adams, to all commanders. An official report of the attack on Pearl Harbor is transmitted to commanders in the Pacific Region.

EXTRA PRIORITY

ALL ARMY CORPS AREA COMMANDERS

Japan opened hostilities in Hawaii at eight o'clock Hawaiian time by air attack apparently from carrier involving approximately fifty Japanese planes stop

Attack still in progress stop

Hangers at Nichols Field and Wheeler Field are in flames and Japanese planes reported as machine gunning over Hickani Field stop

Rumoured one US battleship struck in Pearl Harbor but no confirmation this report stop

Our Army and Navy planes are in the air stop

Manila has also been attacked but no details yet stop

In co-operation with FBI round up all the suspicious characters on your lists stop

Corps Area Commanders will notify manufacturers to take all special measures for protection against sabotage

The Japanese attack fleet sailed towards Hawaii for four days under cover of a weather front which moved at the same speed. At the moment of the first attack the cloud parted to reveal their target. The Japanese assumed it was divine intervention. The attack, in two waves, sank six battleships, three destroyers, three light cruisers and 164 planes.

———

The Japanese attack on Pearl Harbor cost 2,403 American lives. The total was kept from the American newspapers.

———

The calamitous circumstances surrounding the surprise attack on Pearl Harbor led to six wartime investigations, a post-war Congressional inquiry and countless conspiracy theories suggesting prior knowledge of the attack by Roosevelt and/or Churchill. None has been shown to have any substance.

Admiral Yamamoto, who had planned the attack on Pearl Harbor, was opposed to war with America and to the Tripartite Pact. He knew the attack had not been sufficiently successful, the US carriers were at sea and Vice-Admiral Nagumo, who was in charge of the attack, refused to launch a third strike fearing a counter-attack.

There were only two minor attacks on the continental United States during the Second World War. A single Japanese submarine surfaced and opened fire on a military depot in Oregon. Later, a light aircraft took off from the deck of a submarine and dropped incendiaries in a forest in the same state. There were no casualties.

SUNDAY, 14 DECEMBER 1941 – SUB. LT. KAZUO SAKAMAKI, JAPANESE NAVY

Japanese Navy Officer Kazuo Sakamaki survived the stranding of his midget submarine on a coral reef. Sakamaki became the first Japanese prisoner of war and made the following statement.

To a Commanding Officer
from Japanese Naval Officer Kazuo Sakamaki

2. RECORD OF BATTLE

Your honourable 'have' country instituted an economic blockade of Japan, a 'have not' country, refusing to sell us oil, cotton and the like, until we had no choice but natural collapse. Because of this we began diplomatic negotiations with your country, but these ended in failure. Therefore, with a friend, I set out for Pearl Harbor with the purpose of sinking a battleship, but … since the _____ accident was fatal to the submarine, we determined to proceed without hesitation on the surface of the water, and dashing into the harbour, and climbing the gang-way ladder, hoped to leap into the dock and die simultaneously with blowing up the enemy warship just as in olden times, during the Mongol invasion … Later, finally being unable to do anything with the submarine, I swam through the ocean and reached an enemy airport. Due to my exhaustion, I was captured without having time to even fight. And thus my sad fate began.

Due entirely to my inexpert navigation and strategy, my honour as a soldier has fallen to the ground. Thus I betrayed the expectations of our 100,000,000 [people] and became a sad prisoner of war disloyal to my country … I will commit suicide upon my return to my native land. Even though we are unarmed, to bite with teeth and fight to the last is the Japanese spirit …

Showa 16th year [1941], 14th day [month omitted]

KAZUO SAKAMAKI, NAVAL SUB-LIEUTENANT

FRIDAY, 12 DECEMBER 1941 – RADIOMAN 1ST CLASS RAYMOND M. TUFTELAND, US NAVY

Aboard the USS Chicago, Radioman Tufteland heard of the attack on Pearl Harbor. Five days later his ship entered the port and he chronicled the destruction he saw.

USS CHICAGO, PEARL HARBOR, HAWAII

Our force entered Pearl to witness a ghastly sight of sunken ships – oil covered water – wreckage and ruins. We first passed the Nevada which had been beached to prevent sinking. Next one was California – badly damaged and on the bottom. The hull of the Oklahoma then came in sight after having capsized. The Tennessee and West Virginia

103

LEFT: Lt. Cdr. David McCampbell was awarded the Congressional Medal of Honor for shooting down 9 Japanese aircraft in a single mission. He was the US Navy's leading ace with 34 'kills'.

ABOVE: Swastikas displayed on an American fighter aircraft.

LEFT: The Success Slate: the tailplane of a Luftwaffe bomber.

behind her were both damaged. However the team got underway and left the W.Va still on bottom. The Arizona was completely blown up and a twisted mass of iron. Bodies were still being taken from ships and out of water a week after the attack. It was a sight none of us like to remember but must avenge! ...

SUNDAY, 21 DECEMBER 1941 – CPL. JOHN WYATT, BRITISH ARMY

John Wyatt joined the East Surrey Regiment in June 1940. He was posted to their 2nd Battalion, stationed in Alor Star, Northern Malaya. Following the Japanese invasion on 8 December 1941, his unit was amalgamated with the 1st Battalion, Leicestershire Regiment, to form the British Battalion. Corporal Wyatt's letter is an account of the Battalion's operations at Gurun on 14/15 December 1941. After the fall of Singapore, Wyatt became a prisoner of war in Japanese hands until 1945.

SINGAPORE, L/CPL J. WYATT, D. COY, BRITISH BATTALION
DEC. 21, 1941 MALAYA

Dear Mum and Dad,

Hope this finds you as safe and as well as I am at present.

[...] Well mum before I start I would like to give thanks to God at Church for the mercy he has shown, not only to me but to the whole Battalion, 3 times. I have just waited for death but with Gods help I am still here, I have felt all along that with all your prayers God would keep me safe. I will only give you one instance of it: 10 of us were in a trench in a little native village in the Jungle, we were told last man last round, for we were surrounded by Japanese and they were closing in on all sides. Some of the chaps were saying goodbye to each other and I was really frightened at the thought of dying but as the minutes dragged on I resigned myself to it, then all of a sudden three aircraft came over, was they ours? Was they be buggered, down came the bombs all around us. All we could do as we crouched there was to wait for one to hit us but that good old trench saved our lives for it swayed and rocked with the impact, about one minute after they flew off believe it or not 4 tanks rumbled up the road, and gave our positions hell they flung everything at us; grenades, machine guns, but still we crouched in that little trench, we could not return fire for if we showed our heads over the trench the advancing Japs were machine gunning us. All of a sudden we heard a shout, run for it lads, and we run, but that was the last I saw of the Brave Officer who said it. I shall never forget him, as we ran past him, pistol in hand holding them off while we got away. I haven't seen him since.

[...] thank God I am still here, most of the Battalion reached safety but a lot of poor chaps are still missing some of my friends too. [...] We certainly knocked the Japs about while we were there didn't we, we are miles better than them and we

BELOW: A German artillery position on Mt Elbrus in the Caucasus Mountains.

RIGHT: Major-General Dwight D Eisenhower at his London desk. A 1915 graduate from West Point Military Academy, he was Commander of US Forces in the European Theatre of Operations in 1942.

ABOVE: One of the first detachments of US troops to be based in Britain marches in a London square in March 1942. By the war's end over two million US servicemen would have passed through Southampton alone.

The battle of the Coral Sea was the first naval battle to be fought entirely by planes from aircraft carriers, where the opposing ships never sighted one another.

are sorry we won't be able to get another smack at them. I shall have to hurry as the candle is burning out. So I will say good-bye for now. Dorrie xxx Jimmie, George, Mrs. Ward Church, rest of family and neighbours. So please don't worry, God bless you all and keep safe.

Your ever loving son JOHN V xxxxxxxxxxx

P.S. I shall have a lot to tell you when I get home. As usual Jerry is here with the Japs, German pilots and German N.C.O.s. Tell Dorrie that the corporal who wrote to her is missing but safe I think, and my sergeant who wrote to her got shot in the leg and is a prisoner I believe.

SATURDAY, 24 JANUARY 1941 – REAR ADM. RANDELL JACOBS, US NAVY

Official telegram to Mrs Dunlap with the news that her sons Wes and Bud Heidt are considered to have been killed in the attack on Pearl Harbor. Days before the Japanese attack they had both written from the ship the USS Arizona.

WASHINGTON DC

Mrs Genevieve Dunlap

After exhaustive search it has been found impossible to locate your sons, Wesley John Heidt Fireman First Class US Navy and Edward Joseph Heidt Fireman First

Class US Navy and they have therefore been officially declared to have lost their life in the service of their country as of December seventh nineteen forty one x The Department expressed to you its sincerest sympathy
REAR ADMIRAL RANDALL JACOBS,
BUREAU OF NAVIGATION

ABOVE: German artillery fires on enemy positions on the Eastern Front.

TUESDAY, 23 JUNE 1942 – INA KONSTANTINOVA

Motivated by the calls of Stalin for everyone to defend the Russian Motherland she volunteered at the age of 16 to fight as a Partisan against the Germans. Below is an entry from her diary.

KASHIN, NORTH-EAST OF MOSCOW

I haven't written for a long time. So much has happened! I was not mistaken: this copy-book will see a great deal. I particularly remember the events of 19 June. At night a large punitive detachment approached our village very, very close. The exchange of fire continued throughout the night. In the morning, when we woke up, villages burned all around us. Soon the first casualty was brought to me. My hands were covered with blood, then I took this seriously wounded man to a doctor, 6 kms away. When I returned, we had to execute a certain village elder, a collaborator. We went to get him; we read him the sentence and led him to the place of execution. I felt awful.

   In the evening, about eleven, just as I was getting ready to go to bed, another wounded man was brought in. Again I dressed his wounds, and again had to deliver him to a doctor. And the weather was terrible; it was cold, dark, raining, and windy! I dressed warm and we went. My sick man instantly froze; I had to give him at first my rain cape and then my jacket. I had only a blouse on, and was terribly chilled. On the way, the cart broke down and I fixed it, and then we got lost. In short, it took us four hours to get to our destination. I barely had time to warm up a bit when I had to start back. I returned in the morning; I had quite a night!

SUNDAY, 18 OCTOBER 1942 – YITSKHOK RUDASHEVSKI

Yitskhok was 14 years old when the Germans invaded Lithuania in 1941. With her Jewish parents she and all other Jews were forced to move to the ghetto. Not all Jews refused to co-operate with the occupying powers, as she describes.

VILNA, LITHUANIA

Jewish policemen donned official hats. I walk across the street and here go some of them wearing leather jackets, boots and green round hats with glossy peaks and Stars of David. Here goes Smilgovski (an 'officer') in the dark blue hat and a golden Star of David. They march smartly by in unison. (Jackets are being 'loaned' by force in the streets.) They impress you as Lithuanians, as kidnappers. An unpleasant feeling comes over me. I hate from the bottom of my heart, ghetto Jews in uniforms, and how arrogantly they have somehow become such strangers to the ghetto. In me they arouse a feeling compounded of ridicule, disgust and fear. In the ghetto it is said that the reason for the uniforms is that thirty Vilna policemen are riding to the neighbouring towns to set up a ghetto in Oshmene. This is not known for certain.

SEPTEMBER 8–16, 1942 – UNKNOWN JAPANESE SOLDIER

Diary extract written during his time at Guadalcanal.

… Sept 8 Last night the enemy and our fleet fought aggressively at sea.

… Sept 9 Since early morning our planes fought the enemy planes. Saw a plane, which looked like the enemy's, parachute down …

From Sept 9th to 10th Sea battle off the Taivu Point. A ship, which was unidentifiable, caught fire and was burning till about 5:00 am the 10th …

Sept 13 Clear: On the central part of Guadalcanal Island …

From about 5:30 am several planes were flying at low altitude over the surface of the sea and above us so we hid in the jungle in the Tarzan-like shelter. While we were eating breakfast, a big lizard appeared. Its beauty can not be described with words. Its size was about 2 inches around the breast.

Pig hunting is a daily occurrence and today Sgt. Shiraishi caught a pig and Futami caught a chicken.

ABOVE: Scared yet defiant, a small child looks at a German photographer in the occupied town of Poltava.

LEFT: A street market in the occupied town of Kharkov in 1942. As the war wore on ever worsening shortages gave value to the smallest item.

The lizard comes out to eat the pig bones everyday …

Sept 15 … Received a small quantity of wine made from coconut tonight. It was very pleasant.

Sept 16 … Stomach ached from the coconut wine of last night. There is no news of the main force but believed that it is now making tunnels in preparation for general attack finally …

SEPTEMBER 15 TO OCTOBER 11, 1942 – ANOTHER UNKNOWN JAPANESE SOLDIER

Diary extract of a member of a rapidly dwindling group of Japanese soldiers.

… Sept 15th The location of the Brigade could not be found, though searched for it every day. Met Sgt. Lakase from Kumamoto on about 11 am and then followed him. Our food was gone.

Sept 24 Sgt. Takase and 13 men ended the day by eating some kind of potato.

Sept 25 Enemy invaded our bivouac area in the forest. Much to our regret Pvt. lcl Nagata was killed in the battle. At 2 am moved to another position during the night. Accompanied the ammunitions squad, starting today.

Sept 26th Became ill today. Due to the unusually bad weather, to say nothing of the clothings, weapons becoming rusty, and the materials for cleaning them being lost, I, and even my buddies, have never suffered so much from the battle and sickness in my 7 years at war …

Oct 9th Clear. Celebrated our Aoi Jinja Day on the Guadalcanal Island in the South Seas and offered reverence to god. Am getting better every day.

Oct 11th Rain. Unfortunately Sgt. Iwasaki died … in the afternoon. There were 3 of us now …

LATE 1942/EARLY 1943 – CPL. PERRAZZO

Cpl. G. Perrazzo writes to a friend about a fellow Australian's courage.

21 BRIGADE HQ, AIF, NEW GUINEA

[Tom] had to be dragged up the slope of the mountain several hundreds of feet meanwhile his fractured leg was dragging all over the place and catching in the bushes. He fainted many times with pain but did not whimper once … The position was dangerous and he begged them to let him remain where he was and make a safe get-away themselves; this they refused to do and after a stupendous job they got him to safety. It took 3 days to get him down through the mountains.

The battle of Midway was to be the first decisive defeat inflicted on the Japanese by the Americans. A Japanese Task Force for the invasion of Midway island was intercepted, four aircraft carriers were sunk at a loss of 332 aircraft and 3,500 men. The Americans lost the carrier *Yorktown*, 147 aircraft and 307 men.

Forty-two thousand civilians were killed in the Hamburg firestorm of July 1943, following less than an hour of bombing, more than were killed in London during the entire war.

FIVE

TOTAL WAR

1939-45

The Second World War rapidly escalated into a global conflict. Its ferocity soon engulfed more civilians than combatants, and often blurred the line between the two. The war was a maelstrom of death unique in history. Nothing could offer a better definition of 'Total War' than a death toll of fifty million.

The scale of the killing partly reflected the particular hatreds engendered on the Eastern Front and the obscene fanaticism of the Holocaust, but in the main, the intensity of the Second World War was driven by technology.

It was a war like all wars, fought and won according to the potency of the weapons and military resources brought to bear by the protagonists. But, for the first time, the Second World War hinged on the mobility of the weapons and on the scale and speed at which they could be produced. It was a war that could devour vast amounts of territory in highly mobile tanks and armoured infantry. It was a war that could rain devastation from the skies onto any city in the world from dive-bombers and superfortresses. It was a war of all the vast oceans of the world contested by aircraft carriers and torpedo planes and convoys and submarines. And it was a war of long-range communication, heard by everyone on earth, fought by radio and radar, by codes and code-breakers, and by espionage and propaganda.

Behind the fighting armies were even bigger armies of civilians. Oil, steel, aluminium, rubber and countless other scarce resources had to be transformed into the fuel, rifles, shells, tyres, ball-bearings and propellers that

would ultimately determine the outcome of the war. The economics of mass production and the mobility, skill and dedication of civilian labour were as important as the generals' deployment of battle plans, or the courage of the soldier at the front.

Hitler understood the significance of armaments production and the need for resources. Germany had been systematically re-arming itself for war throughout the 1930s and much of the logic behind the need for *Lebensraum* (living space), which obsessed Hitler so much, was a result of the limited natural resources within Germany's borders.

The key to allied wartime production was the huge productive capacity of the United States. Initially, American support for Europe came in the form of 'Cash and Carry'. This allowed France and Britain to pay cash for armaments from America and to transport them to Europe. But America's armed forces had been gradually reduced following the First World War and they were unable and unwilling to engage in any fighting themselves. Most significantly, the bulk of the American people were staunchly isolationist in 1940 and President Roosevelt was running for an unprecedented third term.

It was a source of great relief to the free world when Roosevelt secured his third term in November of that year. A month later, Roosevelt was able to change significantly the basis of American support. Britain was running out of money so 'Cash and Carry' became 'Lend-Lease'. Roosevelt likened it to lending your

ABOVE: Women from a West Country munitions plant are shown how to fire the mortar bombs they manufacture.

neighbour your garden hose to put out a fire. He said that America would become 'the great arsenal of democracy'. 'Lend-Lease' was vital to the outcome of the war. Productivity in the United States increased ten-fold in four years.

Producing weapons of war is one thing, getting them to the right place at the right time is quite another. During the Second World War, the right place was usually thousands of miles away, the right time was invariably tomorrow. For the 'arsenal of democracy' to work effectively, American materials had to be transported across the North Atlantic in massive convoys menaced by 'wolf-packs' of German U-boats trying to

114

obliterate them. For the early years of the war the submarines were in the ascendancy, reaching a climax in early 1943 when allied convoys were losing over 20 per cent of their ships. But the Battle of the Atlantic, as it came to be known, swung in the Allies' favour by increases in naval protection and air support and, in particular, by intelligence penetration of the U-boat communication code. In fact, Allied superiority in code-breaking was of vital importance throughout the war.

In 1939 Germany possessed the world's best machine for creating coded messages. It was called Enigma. Throughout the war, Germany thought that its military signals continued to be transmitted in secret. But, British intelligence had been given two Enigma machines by Polish intelligence officers, who had acquired them before the fall of Poland in 1939. With this vital hardware available to them they were able to unlock the secret German messages by using teams of code-breakers and weeks and weeks of painstaking analysis. It was called Ultra intelligence.

Another vital piece of military intelligence, which significantly influenced the Battle of the Atlantic, was the development of high-frequency direction-finding techniques which allowed convoy support ships and planes to detect U-boats with increasing levels of accuracy. Although shipping losses continued to be high, the Germans had to pay an ever greater price in submarines to sustain them. Eventually the wolf-packs were withdrawn in May 1943.

With millions of men committed to the armed forces, the mass production of weapons could only be achieved by the mobilization of women. In countries spared the horrors of occupation, women had the chance to work in new areas of employment. 'War work' for women

LEFT: American women war-workers making parts for the US Navy's Coronada flying boat at the Consolidated-Vultee aircraft plant, Downey, California.

included, in some cases, administrative and middle management roles, but in the main involved manual labour in munitions factories and in agricultural production. It did represent a shift in women's perception of themselves and to a lesser degree in men's perception of women. But, on the whole, most men expected to have their jobs back when they returned from fighting and that women would go back to home-making.

A similar hypocrisy applied to the wartime experiences of African-Americans. War also meant new employment opportunities for them. This led to a major migration of black Americans from the Old South to the cities of the north. Over a million people made the transition during wartime. But this caused considerable racial tension in the cities. In one of the sad paradoxes of the war, America continued its traditions of segregation, discrimination and racial violence throughout its war with Nazi Germany, whose policies of racial bigotry were so reviled by Allied propaganda. Even in Washington itself, public facilities were segregated throughout the war and African-Americans were unable to vote in most states of the union. The armed forces remained segregated until 1948, despite the fact that almost a million black Americans were in the services by 1945.

Nevertheless, migration north and service for the nation, often overseas, did allow many black Americans at least a psychological break from the centuries-old constraints of slavery and the South. It did much to raise their self-esteem and brought them into contact with other cultures and political traditions.

1939

Aug. 30 The evacuation of children from Paris begins.

Sep. 1 The evacuation of children from London begins.

Sep. 27 An emergency budget in Britain raises the standard rate of income tax by 50 per cent (from five shillings and sixpence to seven shillings and sixpence).

Nov. 4 Roosevelt signs the 'Cash and Carry' bill allowing Britain and France to purchase American weapons.

Nov. 18 German mines sink 60,000 tons of shipping in the North Sea in a single week.

1940

Jan. 8 Food rationing begins in Britain.

July 10 Trade Unions are abolished in Vichy France.

1941

Mar. 11 The Lend-Lease bill is signed in Washington.

Apr. 7 British income tax reaches ten shillings in the pound (50 pence in the pound).

Apr. 10 The rationing of rice is introduced in Japan.

June 1 Clothes rationing begins in Britain.

June 25 Roosevelt establishes the Fair Employment Practices Commission to investigate racial discrimination in employment. He thus prevents a mass march on Washington by African-Americans.

Nov. 13 US Congress amends the Neutrality Act allowing US supply ships to be armed and enter war zones.

Dec. 9 National Service Bill makes single British women aged 20 to 30 subject to military service.

1942

Jan. 10 The Office of War Production is established in America.

Sep. Gasoline rationing is introduced in America. Car production is suspended. 'Liberty' ships go into production.

Oct. 15 Local councils and neighbourhood associations begin to organize food and clothing rationing in Japan.

Oct. Press censorship is introduced in America.

1943

May 3 Part-time work for women aged 18 to 45 is made compulsory for British women.

June 7 The Smith-Connally Act authorizes the American president to be able to seize any factory where strike action could interrupt war production.

June 9 The American Congress introduces 'Pay-As-You-Go' income tax, taken from wages and salaries.

Dec. Some National Service inductees (21,000) are diverted to work in British coal mines. They are called 'Bevin Boys' after Ernest Bevin, Minister for Labour.

1944

Feb. 10 The 'Pay As-You-Earn' system of income tax is introduced in Britain.

July A world conference at Bretton Woods in New Hampshire, USA establishes a world economic system based on fixed exchange rates. The International Monetary Fund and the World Bank are founded.

1945

Aug. 24 American President Harry S. Truman ends the 'Lend-Lease' aid programme.

TUESDAY, 13 MAY 1941 – CLARA EMILY MILBURN

Clara's son Alan has been taken prisoner. While she knew he was alive one letter had not arrived in sequence. Rudolf Hess was to remain imprisoned until 1987 when he was found to have committed suicide in Spandau Prison, Berlin.

BELOW: Miss M Greatorex poses for an official photographer of the British Ministry of Information. She was employed as a machine operator manufacturing spring cases for 17lb field guns.

COVENTRY, ENGLAND

All day I have been thinking of Alan, for a missing letter, dated 17.4.41, arrived this morning. It is the first from Stalag XXXA and describes conditions in the camp, with its underground passages dimly lit, its small windows with no view and the country dull and flat. Most depressing it sounds. But the letter we received the other day says they are in high spirits, and in today's letter he says they are as good a crowd as one could be shut up with. So, since it must be borne, I am glad that this is so and that the food seems good and he had plenty to do.

The great news today is that Rudolf Hess, Hitler's runner-up, who was supposed to have gone out in an aeroplane and been killed, is now known to have landed by parachute in Scotland! A story of the film type it sounded, but apparently it is true. Someone of high standing who knows him has proved that he is the real Rudolf Hess and he is not mentally deranged, nor suffering from any

LEFT: Women railway workers of the C&NW Railroad take a meal break at Clinton, Iowa. They had replaced men as locomotive cleaners.

RIGHT: British women manufacturing rubber dinghies for aircraft.

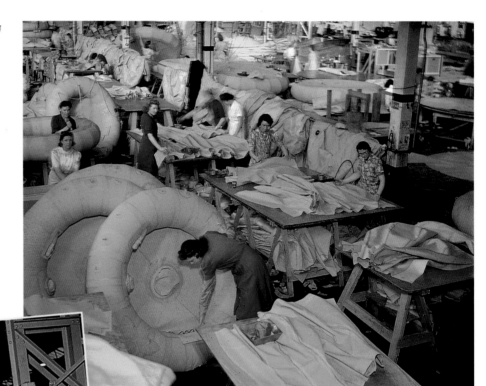

BELOW: A female lathe operator.

disease, as the Germans put forth yesterday. His ankle was injured and he was seen by a crofter to be coming down by parachute in a lonely spot in Scotland. Truly dramatic!

TUESDAY, 1 JULY 1941 – JOHN COLVILLE

'Lord Haw-Haw' was a key player in Goebbels' propaganda war against Britain. Born William Joyce in New York on 24 April 1906, he broadcast throughout the war to Britain with the famous introduction 'Germany Calling, Germany Calling'. Arrested by the British in 1945 he was hanged at Wandsworth Prison on 3 January 1946. His last words in a condemned cell letter of that date were 'Sieg Heil, Sieg Heil'. From Colville's diary it is clear Churchill is anxious about the impact German propaganda is having on British opinion.

LONDON, ENGLAND

The P.M. gave different instructions to me, Rowan and Ismay about the Middle East announcements. He is petrified of a leakage through some foreign Embassy which would enable Lord Haw Haw to be first with the news.

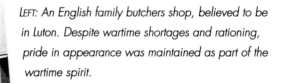

LEFT: An English family butchers shop, believed to be in Luton. Despite wartime shortages and rationing, pride in appearance was maintained as part of the wartime spirit.

BELOW: Flour brought over from North America in convoy is unloaded at a port 'somewhere in the UK'.

LEFT: Bombers of the USAAF share the English countryside with a female farmworker at harvest time.

RIGHT: German prisoners of war were used to help with the harvest in many parts of Britain.

FEBRUARY 1942 – FRANK CURRY, ROYAL CANADIAN NAVY

Curry was Asdic operator on HMCS Kamsack, a corvette escorting convoys across the Atlantic, continually facing the menace of attack by German U-boats.

ATLANTIC

4.2.42 Up anchor at 0400 (no boarding during the night) and sailed with St. Laurent and four other corvettes. Out of Loch Foyle and so off to sea. facing us a rather unpleasant prospect. Feeling pretty grim as we plunge our way out into the Atlantic. Headed north-west, where to, know not we. Heavy seas running, and already our little ship is a mess ...

5.2.42 A weird feeling to see it pitch dark at 0900 and a full moon shining down on us ... we are heading to the north with our large westbound convoy, in the hope of eluding subs; operating steadily, with the seas having leveled off just a little, much to the relief of everyone on board.

6.2.42 Thick fog has settled down around us – rather a queer feeling to be escorting a convoy that is invisible a huge convoy of 73 ships. Suddenly at 1500 we cleared the fog and it was an amazing sight to gaze on our convoy in the brilliant sunshine. Lots of time off watch spent behind the funnel, the gathering place for the Funnel Gang – off watchers.

7.2.42 Sea smooth as silk – there has been trouble close by. We sighted several large pieces of wreckage and then we came upon two machine-gun-riddled life boats, two dead seamen in one – nothing we could do about it – a terrible sight and I feel it very deeply. Action stations in the noon hour and the Rimouski, our old winger, is going at it hot and heavy on the other side of the convoy with a sub contact. No contacts for us, but I feel pretty tense every minute I am operating on the old Asdic set.

8.2.42 Beautiful sunrise as I operated on the 0400-0600 watch. Something to remember, just to sit high on the bridge and gaze out on such a magnificent scene, with brilliant sun coming up in the east and our great convoy steaming quietly on its way, with little corvettes spotted out on all wings. Still smooth as anyone could wish for – everyone amazed and happy about it. We picked up a good sub echo on the Asdic at 1925 and threw four patterns of depth charge at it – crew pretty tense, not to mention one FC.

ABOVE LEFT: *Sir Alexander Fleming discovered penicillin in 1928, but it was only available from 1939.*

120

ABOVE: Construction of Lancaster bombers at the AV Roe & Co plant in Woodford, Essex in 1943.

LEFT: A British steelworker involved in the production of Sten Guns in 1943.

RIGHT: A Royal Navy anti-aircraft gunner probably aboard HMS George V in November 1942.

LEFT: A German U-boat crew member beneath the North Atlantic.

ABOVE: Two ratings aboard HMS Forth in Holy Loch, Scotland, 1942.

9.2.42 A bit rough today, but really nothing to moan about. We are ploughing right ahead with our large convoy and making good progress. We have certainly swung far to the north with this one, and are now well up between Iceland and Greenland … must be method in this madness.

10.2.42 Seas have flattened out again, and we are steaming right along with nothing out of the ordinary for the last couple of days. Just a constant alertness for something to happen …

11.2.42 Still (I repeat still) smooth as smooth. Grand warm sun came out and poured down on us all this long day. If you were trying to convince anyone back home that winter in the north Atlantic was not exactly a picnic, you would have a tough time today. Seems more like a summer cruise in the Caribbean. But we are not complaining a bit …

12.2.42 Does not take long to change. This morning is rather rough and much, much colder. Guess we have moved out of the Gulf Stream and are now getting closer to the dear shores of Newfoundland. Feeling in an awful mood, and I thought I would go raving mad on the 2400-0400 watch. Staggered through it somehow.

BELOW: A stoker aboard a Royal Navy battleship comes up to the deck for air and a glimpse of daylight.

RIGHT: Divine service is held aboard a battleship of the Royal Navy.

America declared itself the 'Arsenal of Democracy' in December 1940 by inaugurating the 'Lend-Lease' policy which granted aid in goods and services to nations fighting Germany, Italy and, eventually, Japan.

WEDNESDAY, 13 MAY 1942 – ABRAHAM LEWIN

German propaganda units continued film production throughout the war. The policy of filming Jews, gypsies and Russian prisoners by the Germans in a manner to endorse their own political message of the Nazi ideology is typically described below in the diary of a Jew in the Warsaw Ghetto.

WARSAW, POLAND

Yesterday the Germans, with the help of the Jewish police, rounded up young Jewish girls, and women both young and old, and also men with and without beards on the street and in particular among the occupants of 38 Dzielna Street. Two lorry-loads of German, air force, SS and men from other units, as well as a smaller vehicle with officers in it, drew up at the entrance of 38 Dzielna Street. First of all they photographed all the young girls – incidentally, they then picked out girls and women who were particularly respectable-looking and expensively dressed. Then they pushed all the Jewish men and women in to the bath-house that is in the corner of the courtyard of the above mentioned building. Once inside they photographed all the women again. Then they forced the men and women to strip completely naked. German officer divided them into pairs made of one from each sex from among the Jews. They matched young girls to old men, and conversely, young boys to old women. Then they forced the two sexes to commit a sexual act. These scenes... were filmed with special apparatus that had been brought in for that purpose.

WEDNESDAY, 13 MAY 1942 – PRIVATE MILTON ADAMS

Adams writes to Warren Hastie, the United States Government's adviser on 'Coloured Affairs', telling of racism rampant in the US army and society at that time. The use of grammar and spelling in the letter below offers an insight into the minimal level of education offered to many African-Americans at that time.

COMPANY B, 240TH QUARTER MASTER'S BATTALION
CAMP LIVINGSTON, LOUISIANA, USA

Dear Mr. W. H. Hastie:

I am private Milton Adams of Co[mpany]B. 24th Q[uarter] M[aster] B[attallion]n of camp Livingston, La. I enlisted in the army Oct 17, 1942, in Chicago,Ill. And since I been in the Army, I have never had any Trouble in the Army or out of it in my life, until I came to Camp Livingston. I am asking for the help of the N.A.A.C.P. And the Crisis. I am not writing anything against the United States Army. But I am going to tell you what the White officers are doing to us races Soldiers down her in camp in Livingston, La. Since they can't very well hang us, they take the next steps, which is court martial, and that is better know as rail-roading. Now you don't stand a chance, before them. They

The Lend-Lease policy transferred 42,000 million dollars of goods and services to the Allies. Forty-five per cent were in munitions, 20 per cent in industrial material, 14 per cent in food and 11 per cent in services.

———

Over 50 per cent of 'Lend-Lease' aid went to Great Britain. About 20 per cent went to the USSR.

———

German and Japanese territorial conquests involved a huge drain on their military resources, but the increased supply of raw materials from conquered lands was dramatically beneficial to their economic production. German supplies of coal increased 60 per cent between 1936 and 1944; iron ore increased 140 per cent. Japan could not have sustained its war effort without the vast oil reserves of southern Asia.

ABOVE: 3 March 1945 – Viareggio, Italy – Men of the 317th Engineer Battalion, 92nd (Negro) Division, probe for mines along a beach. Many complaints were made that African-American servicemen were the victims of continuing and virulent racism in the US military.

are just like a lynch mob with a neggro to hang. Well they do not want you down here in the Army, and I did not ask to come down hear I was sent down hear. Well my trouble starter when they found out that I was from Chicago, and I have had a bad deal ever since I been hear, I have tried to get away from hear, But it was the same old story. When we find some places for you to go, we will let you go. Well my Commanding Officer did not like me because, I ask him not to use the word niggers, and he said I was one of those smart nigger from up north. I was tried once for a offince, and given 30 days and a $12.00 fine. Now after I had finish my sentences, they saide they are going to try me over again. I wish you would look into my case.

I thought they could not try any person a second time for the same offince. I really taken all the punishment I can take I could not get a three day pass or a furlo since I been in the army, until my mother pass away in April. They have just about rob me out of very pay day, for things I have never had. There are so many more case like this, a unfair chance. I don't know what to do now. I don't want do the wrong thing, so I am asking for help. But I am not going to take any more of these unfair trials, because I did three months in the stockade once for something I did not have any thing to do with. It was because I was from Chicago, and thats way every trial I ever had is base on the fact that I come from Chicago. So I whishyou look into this case, because I can prove everything I am telling you. I will look forward to a answer from you in a few days.
Respectfully yours,
Pvt. Milton Adams, Post Stockade, Camp Livingston, La.

Sunday, 28 June 1942 – State Secretary Luther, German Foreign Office

Telegram from Assistant Undersecretary in the Foreign Office, Luther, pertaining to the deportation of Belgian French and Dutch Jews to Auschwitz.

Berlin, Germany

The Chief of Security police and Security Service has imparted the following:

'Beginning in mid-July or early August, as the case may be, it has been planned to transport initially about 40,000 Jews from French occupied territory, 40,000 Jews from the Netherlands, and 10,000 Jews from Belgium to Camp Auschwitz to perform labour. This is to be accomplished by means of daily special trains with a capacity of 1000 persons.

The persons to be affected will be initially Jews able to work, as long as they do not live in mixed marriages and are not nationals of the British Empire, the USA, Mexico, enemy countries in central and south America or neutral and allied countries.'

Comments at everybody's earliest convenience are requested.

Luther

Sunday, 5 July 1942 – Anne Frank

Anne Frank, by now 13 years old, left Frankfurt, Germany with her family, to flee the horrors of Nazi anti-Semitism. After the German occupation of Holland in 1940 increasing Nazi repression caused many Jews to consider going into hiding. She soon began writing her diary to a fictitious friend and confidante, Kitty.

The convoy method of protecting large groups of merchant ships with a military escort was a major factor ensuring the Allied victory. Ships moving in convoy were four times more likely to avoid sinking by enemy attack than those travelling independently.

———

The Japanese made little use of convoys, or used the method in numbers too small to be effective. As a consequence, they had lost over 90 per cent of their merchant fleet by the end of the war.

In the Battle of the Atlantic, 70 per cent of all Allied convoy losses were inflicted by U-boats. Admiral Dönitz, commander of the U-boat fleet, wanted 300 submarines in order to kill the supply of goods from America. In August 1940 he had only 27 boats available. By the winter of 1943, the number was over 400.

AMSTERDAM, NETHERLANDS

Dear Kitty,

Father has been home a lot lately. There's nothing for him to do at the office; it must be awful to feel you're not needed. Mr Kleiman has taken over Opekta, and Mr Kugler, Gies & Co., the company dealing in spices and spice substitutes that was set up in 1941.

A few days ago, as we were taking a stroll around our neighbourhood square, Father began to talk about going into hiding. He said it would be very hard for us to live cut off from the rest of the world. I asked him why he was bringing this up now.

'Well, Anne,' he replied, 'you know that for more than a year we've been sending our clothes, food and furniture to other people. We don't want our belongings to be seized by the Germans. Nor do we want to fall into their clutches ourselves. So we'll leave of our own accord and not wait to be hauled away.'

'But when, Father?' he sounded so serious that I felt scared.

'Don't you worry. We'll take care of everything. Just enjoy your carefree life while you can.'

That was it. Oh, may these sombre words not come true for as long as possible. The doorbell's ringing, Hello's here, time to stop.

YOURS, ANNE

MONDAY, 8 MARCH 1943 – 1ST LT. SCHWARTZ, SS

Memorandum to the Main Office for the Economy and Administration from SS 1st Lt. Schwartz describing the fate of Jewish deportees from Berlin and Breslau ('Operation Factory') in Auschwitz.

AUSCHWITZ, POLAND

The following prisoner transports arrived on March 5 and 7:

Transportation from Berlin, arrival March 5, 1943, total strength 1,128 Jews, 389 men were assigned for work (Buna), and 96 women. 151 men and 492 women and children received special treatment. Transport from Breslau, arrival March 5, 1943, total strength 1,405 Jews. 406 were assigned for work (Buna) 190 women. 125 men and 684 women and children received special treatment. Transport from Berlin, arrival March 7, 1943, total strength 690 including 25 prisoners in protective custody. 153 men and 25 prisoners in protective custody were assigned for work (Buna), and 65 women. 30 men and 417 women and children received special treatment.

SIGNED: SCHWARTZ

SS FIRST LIEUTENANT

Radar, with High Frequency Direction Finding and the breaking of the U-boat communications code, was vital to keeping the U-boats at bay in 1943 and led to German defeat in the Atlantic.

ABOVE: *Petty Officer Hedley Charles Woodley aboard HM Submarine Tribune. The photograph was taken as a publicity shot in 1942 for the British Ministry of Information film Close Quarters, released in 1943.*

RIGHT: *A shot from the conning tower of HM Submarine Tribune off Scotland in September 1942.*

WEDNESDAY, 19 JULY 1944 – ROSEY NORWALK

American Red Cross Volunteer Rosey Norwalk crossed the Atlantic on the Queen Mary. Converted to wartime service as a troopship, the ship was a prime U-boat target.

BELOW: Muslims parade to celebrate the opening of a new Mosque and Islamic Cultural Centre in Peel Street, Butetown, Cardiff. 1943.

JOURNAL, MID-ATLANTIC

Almost sure we're close to landing. First few days we must have gone south away from regular shipping lanes, as suddenly warmth and my idea of Bermuda blue water was everywhere. For a short time flying fish leaped and at night phosphorescence sparkled the waters. The Queen is so fast she doesn't travel in convoy as she can outrun anything. To evade Nazi U-boats trying to angle in on her, she zigs and zags every so often as she speeds through the water. This huge, high ship going full throttle and heeling over just when you least expect it sometimes interrupts card games, meals and quite a few stomachs. I feel great – maybe it's all in what you anticipate. One of our group turned pasty shortly after we got aboard and suffered premature mal de mer before the ship even sailed. We all had to reassure her that we were still in New York harbour, but it was a blackout so we couldn't let her look out to prove it.

A ship's officer let it slip that U-boats have a real campaign on to zero in on the Queens (the Mary is also a troop carrier). Now that our Allied troops

RIGHT: Refugees from Plymouth at the Chaim Weizmann Home at Tapley Park, Plymouth in October 1942.

are pressing forward off the invasion beaches and the war gets more desperate for Hitler, it's crucial for his U-boats to hit these two ships that carry so many thousands of troops each crossing. And that's why we're taking an unusually circuitous route. Rumours pass around quickly and regularly when there's a submarine alert on. Yesterday it was so reassuring to spot, way off, the famous old Aquitania as we crossed paths in mid-ocean, her four stacks silhouetted against the sky. And later to see a Navy Patrol visible on the horizon. Eloise, a perky redhead from Westport, was particularly glad to spot the patrol as she found out whilst talking with another ship's officer that there are at least 14,000 troops aboard each trip, but only enough lifeboats and floats to take care of 5,000.[...]

FRIDAY, 20 OCTOBER 1944 – ROSEY NORWALK

Rosey confides in her journal of the sexual promiscuity that five years of war had brought to a London landmark.

SOUTHAMPTON, ENGLAND

JOURNAL

Maybe someday I'll tell Mom and Dad about the problems Ski and I had in getting back to our billets from Rainbow Corner [...] because we've only seen Piccadilly Circus in daylight we didn't realise what a flesh market it is in the middle of the night and how dumb we were to tackle it unescorted. The blackout was so complete it was hard to distinguish anything, and the Circus was absolutely jammed with raucously noisy troops and females pushing and elbowing through the mob.

Dumb us – we'd gone over to Piccadilly without a thought, assuming our uniforms would protect us, as usual. Almost without exception we've found our Red Cross uniforms ensure we're treated with respect and courtesy. But in that pitch black madhouse of jostling people we were just two more figures to be bargained with. Each time we got up courage to shine our torch towards what we hoped would be a Tube entrance or cab stand, all we succeeded in doing was getting grabbed and invited – think pressed in all ways – to do all sorts of things.

[...] I shone my torch down an entranceway I was sure would be a Tube entrance but it was only a recessed doorway in which stood two couples (how would Mother say it politely?) coupling.

Ski gasped aloud. 'Can you do it standing up, Rosie?'

How would I know, I thought. 'Shut up Ski!,' I said, 'and keep walking!'

At long last we managed to literally stumble on an entrance to the Tube [...]

After seeing Piccadilly Circus in full midnight bloom, I think I understand better the Brits' favourite lament these days, 'The Yanks are overpaid, oversexed, and over here.'

But even in that total madness, the torch picked out more than American uniforms.

The Arctic convoys were vital to the supply of the Soviet Union. However, in June 1942, a disastrous fate awaited convoy PQ17. Only 11 of the 37 ships that left Iceland made it to the Soviet Union: 4,000 trucks, 430 tanks and 2,500 aircraft were lost, along with 153 sailors.

The German war effort increasingly relied on forced labour, drawn from prisoners-of-war and coerced civilians. By 1944 they represented 24 per cent of the workforce (over seven million people).

———

The Japanese also used forced labour in large quantities, as had Stalin since the early 1930s.

LEFT: An American airman reflects on a field of English poppies, June 1944.

BELOW: Wing Commander Guy Gibson, VC, DSO+Bar, DFC+Bar near Scampton on 22 July 1943. Two months earlier he had led 617 Squadron 'The Dam Busters' on a raid on the Moehne and Eder dams.

LEFT: The all purpose American Jeep displays its ability to be a washstand.

BELOW: Sgt Robert Casey enjoys tinned pineapple at Hollandia, New Guinea, 1944.

ABOVE: Cpl Jack Frutt sleeps on Sgt Ed Bartlett in New Guinea.

RIGHT: Laundry day at the US 320th Bomb Group base in Sardinia, 1944.

SIX

THE TIDE TURNS

SEPTEMBER 1942–JUNE 1944

There are many claims to the title, 'the turning point of the war' and Hitler made numerous costly strategic errors, but the Battle of Stalingrad was such a needless calamity, on such a massive scale, that no other single encounter ranks with the significance of the events on the Volga between August 1942 and February 1943. The city became the symbolic crux of the entire war. Two mighty armies fought hand-to-hand, street-by-street, building-by-building.

As always, Hitler wanted everything, no matter how unrealistic. He wanted Stalin's great city and the oil-fields of the Caucasus. In the end, he got neither. Once again, his army got within a few kilometres of both, but

BELOW: Pilots of 417 Squadron, RCAF, consult maps before an operation on an improvised desk in the Tunisian Desert, April 1943.

stubborn resistance, crucial mistakes and a constant supply of seemingly endless Soviet reinforcements were his undoing. The intense close-quarters fighting in Stalingrad became legendary, as did the massive surrender of the 91,000 strong remnants of the German Sixth Army. The Germans had reaped a whirlwind by their brutality as they had advanced through eastern Europe. Now it would be the Soviets' turn. Of the 91,000 prisoners, only 6,000 made it back to Germany at the end of the war.

But the German line on the Eastern Front was never broken after Stalingrad, they simply made an orderly and disciplined retreat in the face of overwhelming numbers. The Battle of Kursk in July 1943 was an exception, where Hitler hoped for a spectacular tank victory to throw the Red Army into disarray. But after ten days of intense fighting, and hundreds of tanks lost on both sides, the Soviets still held sway. Hitler was reported to have said to one of his generals after Stalingrad, 'The God of War has gone over to the other side'.

There was also a significant reversal for Hitler in North Africa at the end of 1942 following the Anglo-American landings in French North Africa during Operation Torch. Although the fighting was on a considerably smaller scale, the Battle of Alamein in October was a much-needed Allied victory against the German army. It represented a major morale boost and the symbolic turning of the tide in the Mediterranean Theatre.

Rommel's Afrika Korps (by now re-named as the Panzer Army Africa) was heavily out-numbered by

ABOVE: A Lockheed-Hudson flies over Egypt in the summer of 1942.

Montgomery's Eighth Army of British, Australian and New Zealand troops at El Alamein. Montgomery had twice as many tanks and infantry and much better supplies of fuel. It was a battle of attrition where dozens of Allied tanks were lost in exhausting Rommel's limited supplies. Despite yet another futile order from Hitler to stand firm, Rommel was eventually allowed to withdraw. But it was only the beginning of a long retreat across Libya.

The third significant turning point in the land war in 1943 came in the Pacific Islands. In August 1942, the Americans had had to make an emergency marine assault on the island of Guadalcanal in the Solomon Islands. The Japanese had been rapidly constructing an airstrip which would have threatened the vital supply route to Australia. The landing on 7 August was highly successful, but Japanese reinforcements arrived in large numbers and a further six months of bitter fighting ensued, both on land and at sea, until the island fell in February 1943. For the Americans, it became a crash course in jungle warfare at a cost of almost 2,000 American dead and 24,000 Japanese.

It was the beginning of a long and deadly journey to Tokyo. Three thousand miles and hundreds of islands lay between the Solomons and Japan. There was also a high price to be paid by anyone of Japanese descent in America. At the outbreak of the war in the Pacific there were 130,000 of them, mainly living in California. Most of them were native-born American citizens. Nevertheless, the 'Nisei', as they were called, were rounded up, their property sold at the lowest prices and then they were interned in camps throughout America. The internees included at least one decorated First World War veteran. A formal apology and limited compensation were not forthcoming from the US Government until 1988.

Much the same fate befell Germans and Austrians living in Britain, despite the fact that most of them were here because they were anti-Nazi or Jewish. Internment was one of the many restrictions on civil liberties imposed by the Allies because of the exigencies of war.

The next critical step in Europe was the Allied invasion of Italy, begun off Sicily in July. Mussolini's demise followed quickly and the Italians' flimsy commitment to the war evaporated immediately. But the Germans were there in numbers. When the Americans landed on the beaches of Salerno in September, it was a bloody battle and an ominous prelude to the dreadful scenes to come on D-Day. The landings at Anzio in January of the following year were a similar near-disaster. The invasion force became besieged and was pinned down for four months. It would take until mid-summer for the Allies to fight their way to Rome.

In northern Europe, Germany was rapidly losing its air power. Over 4,000 German fighters were lost during the first months of 1944. Allied bombing of airfields, factories and cities continued with ever-greater intensity. In March, 27,000 tons of bombs were dropped on German industry, including the Mercedes Benz plant which was seriously damaged. At the end of March there was a massive raid on Berlin which caused substantial destruction to major parts of the city. Germany was, slowly but surely, being bled to death. However, for the Allies there was a heavy price to pay. Casualty rates among Allied aircrew

LEFT: A setting sun over Wormingford on 11 December 1944 highlights the vapour trails of aircraft.

were frightening. On just one raid, on a single night, more British airmen (over 500) were lost than during the entire Battle of Britain.

As Germany's ultimate fate became more and more apparent, Hitler became ever more impatient about the progress being made in exterminating the Jews of Europe. When Germany took control of Hungary in March, ss officer Adolf Eichmann moved in to extend the 'Final Solution' to the Jews of Hungary. By May, 140,000 had been transported to the gas chambers of Auschwitz. At nearby Birkenau, four separate gas chambers were in operation, sometimes murdering 4,000 people a day for more than two years. Entire communities met their deaths at Birkenau, including the 40,000 Jews of Salonika in Greece and the 10,000 strong community of Bialystok in Poland. To the shame of the authorities in many parts of Europe, the local police and civil service actively participated in the transportation of their own Jewish nationals and Jewish refugees to the death camps.

From mid-1944 onwards, the war became a race against time: a race to beat Hitler before he could complete his 'Final Solution', a race to beat him before he could develop some kind of appalling weapon and a race to beat him as quickly as possible so that resources could be switched to the Pacific to hasten the defeat of Japan. The key to winning the race was the biggest seaborne invasion force in history. Among the many remarkable things about it, the Germans had no idea it was happening. The Normandy landings on D-Day were the beginning of the end for Adolf Hitler and National Socialism.

SEPTEMBER 1942–JUNE 1944

1942

Sep. 18 Soviet reinforcements reach the centre of Stalingrad to bolster the defenders in hand-to-hand fighting in the streets.

Oct. 23 The beginning of the (second) battle of El Alamein in North Africa.

Nov. 4 Rommel retreats at El Alamein, pursued by Montgomery.

Nov. 11 Hitler orders the occupation of Vichy France.

Nov. 13 In North Africa, Tobruk falls to the British.

Nov. 19 Soviet counter-attacks around Stalingrad encircle the German army.

Dec. 19 British and Indian troops attack in Burma.

1943

Jan. 2 The German withdrawal from the Caucasus begins.

Jan. 31 Field Marshal Von Paulus and his German army surrender in Stalingrad.

Feb. 8 The Red Army retakes Kursk.

Feb. 9 US forces capture Guadalcanal.

Feb. 14 The Soviets retake Rostov, and two days later, Kharkov.

Feb. 18 Wingate's 'Chindits' (British and Gurkhas) begin operations behind enemy lines in Burma.

Feb. 25 'Round the clock' Allied bombing of Germany begins.

Apr. 19 The uprising in the Warsaw Ghetto begins.

May 13 The German army in Tunisia surrenders.

May 16 The 'Dam-buster' raid breaches two dams in the Ruhr.

July 4 The beginning of the battle of Kursk. The biggest tank battle in history.

July 10 The Allied invasion of Sicily begins.

July 20 The Germans are pushed back at Kursk. The last German offensive on the Eastern Front is over.

July 25 The king of Italy dismisses Mussolini as Prime Minister and has him arrested.

Sep. 3 Italy surrenders unconditionally.

Sep. 9 The Allies land at Salerno in southern Italy. The Germans retreat to the Gustav Line, north of Naples.

Sep. 15 Mussolini proclaims a new republic after being released from prison by a German SS commando unit under the command of Otto Skorzeny.

Sep. 25 The Soviet army retakes Smolensk.

Oct. 1 British forces occupy Naples.

Nov. 1 American forces land on Bougainville in the Solomons.

Nov. 6 The Soviets retake Kiev.

1944

Jan. 20 The RAF drops 2,000 tons of bombs on Berlin.

Jan. 22 The Allies land at Anzio in Italy.

Jan. 27 The Red Army breaks the siege of Leningrad.

Apr. 2 The Soviets enter Romania.

May 18 Monte Cassino falls to the Allies at the fourth attempt.

June 4 The Allies enter Rome.

LEFT: Three Mark B Avro Lancaster bombers of the RAF from 44 Squadron, based at Waddington, photographed on 29 January 1942: W 4125 (KM-W) piloted by Sgt Colin Watt of RAAF; W 4162 (KM-Y) being flown by Pilot Officer TG Hackney – he was subsequently killed when flying with 83 Squadron; W 4187 (KM-S) flown by Pilot Officer JDVS Stephens, DFM – 2 nights later he was killed during a raid on Wismar.

TUESDAY, 20 JANUARY 1942 – THE FINAL SOLUTION

Protocol of the conference held in a lakeside villa at Berlin-Wannsee where the plan for the 'Final Solution of the Jewish Question' was co-ordinated.

BERLIN-WANNSEE, GERMANY

Top Secret

30 COPIES, 16TH COPY

Protocol.

[…] SS Lieutenant General Heydrich, Chief of Security Police and Security Service, opened the meeting by informing everyone that the Reich Marshal [Goering] had put him in charge of preparations for the final solutions of the Jewish questions. The Reich Marshal's request that a draft be submitted to him with regard to the organizational, functional and material consideration in connection with the final solution of the European Jewish question requires that all central agencies directly concerned with these problems first meet together in order to coordinate their lines of action.

The authority for processing the final solution to the Jewish question lies centralized in the hands of the Reichsführer-SS , head of the German Police (Head of Security Police and Security service), regardless of geographic boundaries. […]

In the course of the final solution the Jews are to be sent in a suitable manner and under appropriate direction to do labour in the east. Separated by sexes, those Jews able to work will be led in large labour columns into these areas while building roads. In the process, large numbers will undoubtedly drop away through natural attrition. The final remainder that conceivably will still be around and that undoubtedly constitutes the sturdiest segment will have to be dealt with accordingly as it represents a natural selection which, when left at liberty, has to be seen as a germ cell of a new Jewish development. (See the lesson history teaches.) […]

During the progress of the final solution project, its basis, as it were, should be the Nuremberg Laws, whereby the solution of mixed marriages and mixed parentage [racially speaking] must likewise be a prerequisite for the definitive settlement of the problem. […]

With regard to the question of how much the evacuation of the Jews would be affecting economic life, Undersecretary Neumann stated that Jews presently working in enterprises essential to the war effort could not be evacuated until they could be replaced. […]

140

The German army actually entered the city of Stalingrad on 12 September. By the 31st, they had taken 70 per cent of the city. But the Soviets were able to filter in a constant supply of fresh troops. Significantly, the German flanks were protected by Romanian and Italian army groups which didn't perform well.

— — —

At one stage of the Battle of Stalingrad, on 27 September, German tanks gained sufficient ground to allow the German flag to be raised over the Communist Party building. Hitler thought victory was imminent, but it never came.

When the Allies launched their attack at El Alamein, Erwin Rommel was on leave in Germany. The German commander, General Stimme, died from a heart attack on the day of the battle.

In conclusion there was a discussion about the various types of possible solutions. Here both Gauleiter Dr Alfred Meyer and Undersecretary Dr. Bühler took the position that in connection with the final solution preparatory measures be carried out at once in the occupied territories, but in such a way as to avoid that the population [of non-Jews] there become apprehensive.

The Chief of Security Police and Security Service (SD) terminated the conference with the request that all participants in today's deliberations give him their cooperation in implementing the tasks connected with the [final] solution.

FRIDAY, 27 FEBRUARY 1942 – MARY BERG

Mary Berg (pseudonym) describes how shootings have now become very frequent at the ghetto exits.

POLAND

Usually they are perpetrated by some guard who wants to amuse himself. Every day, morning and afternoon, when I go to school, I am not sure whether I will return alive. I have to go past two of the most dangerous German sentry posts: at the corner of Zelazna and Chlodna Streets near the bridge, and at the corner of Krochmalna and Grzybowska Streets. At the latter place there is usually a guard who has been nicknamed 'Frankenstein,' because of his notorious cruelty. Apparently this soldier cannot go to sleep unless he has had a few victims to his credit; he is a real sadist. [...] This morning on my way to school, as I was approaching the corner of Krochmalna and Grzybowska Streets, I saw a familiar figure, torturing some rickshaw driver whose vehicle had passed an inch closer to the exit than the regulations permitted. A yellowish liquid dripped from his mouth to the pavement. Soon I realized that he was dead, another victim of the German sadist. The blood was so horribly red and the sight of it completely shattered me.

SEPTEMBER TO OCTOBER 1942 – CHIEF ADMINISTRATOR K.

Extracts from the letters of Chief Administrator K., head of sections 1 and 2 under the Commander of Security Police and the SD in Kiev, to his wife.

After Hitler decided to occupy Vichy France, he lost the opportunity to absorb the French fleet into the German navy when over 40 ships were scuttled by the French in Toulon harbour.

KIEV, UKRAINE

As this war, in our opinion, is a Jewish war, they are the first to feel its impact. So everywhere in Russia, where the German soldier appears, there are no Jews any more. You can imagine that it takes some time for me to get it done. Do not talk with Frau Kern about this. I am also ill (diarrhoea, temperature, fever). Everybody has to go through it here.

[...]

LEFT: Before every mission, a flag ceremony was held at Luftwaffe airbases. The North African Desert was no exception. 1941.

RIGHT INSET: A German motorcycle and sidecar in the dust of the desert, 1942.

RIGHT: British prisoners of war await their fate as prisoners of Rommel's Afrika Korps, 1942.

I am lucky because, due to our hard work, we were allowed to buy additional food. To buy is not the appropriate word – you cannot buy anything for money, you have to barter. By chance we are possessing some clothes, which are in great demand. We get everything here. The things belonged to people who are now dead. You do not need to send me any clothes …

I already wrote you about the shooting and that I could not display any weakness. Generally speaking, they explained that finally a good fellow has been sent to occupy the post of the Chief Administrator, while the former one had been a coward. This is how they judge people here. Quite differently from the way we do it at home. But you can trust your daddy. He is always thinking about you and never shoots excessively. …

Everything would be fine if it was not for the shooting. It was 96 again this morning. I am still excited. The children want to know whether I eat fruit here? I just got hold of several apples but with great difficulty.
[ZENTRALE STELLE LUDWIGSBURG. 204 AR- Z 82/59.]

8 NOVEMBER 1942 TO 3 FEBRUARY 1943 – L/CPL. HEINZ W.

Entries from the diary of the German Lance-Corporal Heinz W. on the situation in Stalingrad before he was taken prisoner. Heinz was working as a cartographer at the headquarters of a pioneer battalion.

GERMAN ARMY, STALINGRAD, USSR
8.11.1942/9.11.42.
On the 9.11 we go to the centre of Stalingrad to bring some logs for the construction of the bunker. The impression from Stalingrad is terrible. A few stone buildings which had been there were razed to the ground during the air raid. Wooden buildings had been dismantled by the infantry to build bunkers, so that Stalingrad is completely in ruins. One can say Stalingrad does not exist any more. It is 15 degrees below zero.
10.11.42. Today we also went to Stalingrad for wood. It is very difficult to find good wood for construction. 19 degrees frost.
11.11.42. Today there was an attack against the Russians, holding the northern part of the city. In the morning we went to the brick factory for bricks, and at lunch – to the Central Station for wood. Frost 15 degrees.
22.11.42. The Soviet village of Krasny was abandoned by us and immediately captured by the Russians. About 20 aircraft and gasoline/supplies/were blown up at an airfield. Now we are moving along the road towards the Don. In the darkness we lose our division and wander around. Russians are everywhere! As the road is under enemy fire, we are accompanied by tanks. This time we are encircled.

The Japanese defeat on Guadalcanal was a decisive victory for the Americans, but the ferocious defence by the exhausted, diseased and outnumbered Japanese confirmed the worst of American fears about the difficulties of removing the Japanese from their conquered territories.

144

RIGHT: A German infantry platoon after the capture of the Stalingrad tractor factory in the northern part of the city on 15 October 1942.

BELOW: Stalingrad residents in German captured territory come out of hiding amidst the almost total devastation of their city in October 1942.

During the naval battle for Guadalcanal the American cruiser *Juneau* was sunk. So fierce was the explosion when the *Juneau* was hit that another American ship, the *Helena*, fled the scene thinking no-one could possibly have survived the blast. In fact, 140 members of the crew of 700 had survived, but were stranded in the water for a week. Only ten survived.

[...]

2.12–4.12.42. This weather deprive our life of any joy. Moreover we have a bad bunker to live. Men are sent to look for firewood. From time to time enemy artillery is shelling our village. ...

31.12.42. The last day of 1942 began. To our great joy we received some bread and chocolate as an addition to the ration. We have a bottle of schnapps, cookies, and good bean coffee for the New Year's Eve. As we have expected, the Russian started attacking at 20.00 in the northern part of Stalingrad and at Spartakovka. At 22.00 we heard tremendous thunder. But it was our artillery this time. In spite of anything, we had a good party to celebrate the beginning of 1943! Of course everybody was thinking about home. There were 9 dead, 23 wounded and 4 missing in the 3rd company.

1.01.43. At 7.30 we all went from our bunker to Gorodishche for sanitary disinfection.

17.01.43. The company had been reduced to 3 persons from 1 officer and 55 soldiers. Senior Lieutenant Rost returned wounded. It is his seventh wound (sixth in Stalingrad)—

18.01.43/19.01.43. The map of the positions and minefields is nearly completed. The terrible cold has weakened. There is absolutely no bread for three days. ...

26.01.43. In the darkness we go further north. We learned that there should be a division somewhere near the tractor factory. So, we are getting through to the northern part of Stalingrad. After a long search we finally found the headquarters, situated in a wet basement.

27.01.43. After a terribly cold night we went to another place – a heating tunnel leading to the tractor factory. Strong artillery fire and aircraft day and night.

28.01.43–1.02.43. We stayed lying down in this heating basement. Further resistance is useless. This fact was recognized by the command of the northern part, the 11th corps, after the surrender of the southern part of Stalingrad on the 29.01. The order for surrender came next morning (General Strecker).

2.02.43. We laid down our weapons in a pile before the entrance, raised a white flag and waited to be taken prisoner. At 9.00 first Russian soldiers came and led us away. We passed the village, the northern cut-off position, then went north all the time. This march continued all the following night.

3.02.43. In the morning, tired to death, we came to a big built-up area. The battalion headquarters men were still keeping together. We were quartered in a big hall. It is terrible that I cannot send a note to my parents. There were 400 of us lying in that hall without light or air. Soon the lice will eat us up, there are hundreds of them on us. Our daily food rations: 400 grams of bread and half a litre of soup.

ABOVE: A Stalingrad woman cooks on the ruins of a stove in German captured territory, October 1942.

THURSDAY, 14 JANUARY 1943 – ALBERT —, GERMAN ARMY OFFICER

The letter of a German officer, sent from Stalingrad by field mail.

STALINGRAD, USSR

Dear uncle!

[…] By a happy chance, I received mail from home again, though it was from last year, and there was the news of your promotion in that letter.

Mail occupies a painfully important place in our soldiers' life. Most of last year's mail have not reached us yet, not to mention the whole bundle of Christmas letters. But in our present situation this kind of misfortune is understandable. You probably know what happened to us; the picture is not rosy, but probably we have already past the critical phase. Every day the Russians make a hullabaloo at some section of the front, throw an enormous number of tanks, accompanied by armed infantry, into action, but their success is small in comparison with their efforts, sometimes it is even negligible.

These battles, involving heavy losses, resemble the fighting of World War I. Material and masses of troops – these are the Russians' idols, and they want to gain a decisive advantage by these means. But their attempts break down against the stubborn fighting spirit and the inexhaustible defensive strength at our positions.

The everyday exploits of our infantry are beyond all description. It is a lofty song of gallantry, bravery and endurance. We have never been waiting for spring as eagerly, as we are waiting for it here. Soon the first half of January will be over, in

The casualties of the *Juneau* included the five Sullivan brothers from Iowa; all in their twenties. All five brothers were among the 140 initial survivors, but none was among the 10 who made it out of the water.

February the situation will still be difficult, but then there will be a turning point – and a big success.

Well, I am finishing now.

My best regards.

ALBERT.

THURSDAY, 4 FEBRUARY 1943 – 'REPORTS FROM WITHIN THE REICH'

Reports about the reactions of the German population to Stalingrad.

147

NO.356, SECURITY SERVICE (SD)

Reports about the termination of the Battle of Stalingrad have shaken the entire people once again to its depth. The speeches of January 30 and the proclamation of the Führer have taken a backseat in view of this event, and play a lesser role in serious conversations on the part of our fellow Germans, than do a number of questions connected with the events at Stalingrad. First of all it is the number of casualties [*Blutoper*] which the population wants to know. Conjunctures fluctuate between 60,000 and 300,000 men. It is being assumed that the great majority of those who fought at Stalingrad have perished.

Regarding those troops who have become prisoners of the

BELOW: Air-Chief Marshal, Sir Arthur T 'Bomber' Harris. Photographed in his office in June 1943, he was responsible for maintaining the policy of aerial bombardment of Germany's cities to demoralise the civilian population.

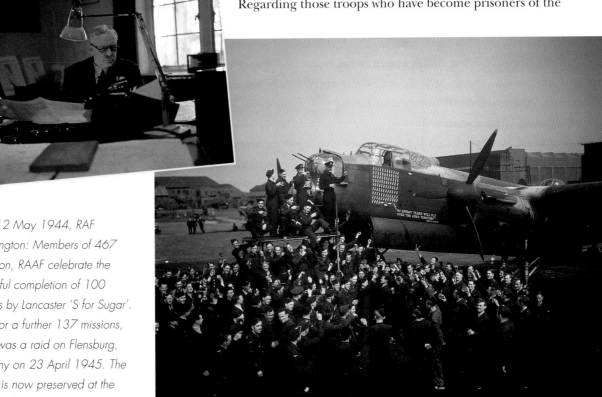

RIGHT: 12 May 1944, RAF Waddington: Members of 467 Squadron, RAAF celebrate the successful completion of 100 missions by Lancaster 'S for Sugar'. Flying for a further 137 missions, its last was a raid on Flensburg, Germany on 23 April 1945. The aircraft is now preserved at the RAF Museum, Hendon.

LEFT: USAAF bombers release their payload over Germany. 1945.

Russians there are two popular conceptions. On the one hand there are those who say that imprisonment is worse than death because they are bound to treat those soldiers who have fallen into their hands alive in an inhumane manner. Others believe in turn how fortunate it is that not all of them have perished; this way there remains the hope that some of them might eventually return to the homeland. Especially the relatives of those who fought at Stalingrad suffer much under this ambiguous situation and the uncertainty that results from it.

Furthermore, large segments of the population are debating whether the developments at Stalingrad were inevitable and whether the immense sacrifices were necessary. Our fellow Germans are specifically concerned with the question whether the retreat to Stalingrad was at the time promptly recognised. Air reconnaissance should have spotted the concentration of Russian armies that were then moving against Stalingrad.

ABOVE: P-47 pilots of the 56th Fighter Group at a briefing at Halesworth, England in January 1944.

Furthermore, the question is being discussed why the city was not evacuated when there was still time.

The third issue around which the conversations of our fellow Germans resolve right now is the importance of the Battle of Stalingrad seen in the context of the war as a whole. [...]

LEFT: A member of the USAAF savours the joys of English life: fish and chips out of a newspaper.

The rising in the Warsaw Ghetto lasted for almost a month despite the fact that the defenders only had pistols, grenades and Molotov cocktails to hold off an SS unit of 3,000 men with heavy armour. About 50 members of ZOB (the Jewish Fighting Organisation) escaped through the sewers. 14,000 Jews died in the rising, but they did manage to take 200 of the German and Polish police with them.

TUESDAY, 16 FEBRUARY 1943 – SERGEANT CARL GOLDMAN

An aerial gunner on a B-17 Flying Fortress attached to the Eighth Air Force in England, Goldman wrote the following letter to his family. It was marked 'To be opened in case of casualty only'. Sergeant Goldman was lost in action over Western Europe.

UNITED STATES ARMY AIR FORCE (USAAF), ENGLAND

Dear Mom, Pop, Frances, Edith, Marion, Leon and Aaron:

Am going on a raid this afternoon or early in the morning. There is a possibility I won't return. In any event, please do not worry too much about me as everyone has to leave this earth one way or another and this is the way I have selected.

I was not forced to go to gunnery school and even after I arrived overseas I could have gotten off combat had I chosen to do so.

If after this terrible war is over, the world emerges a saner place to live; if all nationalities are treated equal; pogroms and persecutions halted, then, I'm glad I gave my efforts with thousands of others for such a cause.

Wish I had time to write more, but sometimes the less said the better, so goodbye – and good luck – always.

CARL

THURSDAY, 18 MARCH 1943 – HEINZ KNOKE, *LUFTWAFFE*

Heinz Knoke was a German fighter pilot on Germany's northern coast based at Jever. Attacking USAAF bombers he witnesses his friend and fellow officer, Lt. Dieter Gerhard, crash into the North Sea, shot down by the aircrew of a Flying Fortress. He awaits news of his possible rescue...

BELOW: A USAAF pilot awaits his next mission.

JEVER, GERMANY

[...]

I open fire on a Liberator from below. It immediately starts burning and sheers off to the right as it falls away from the formation. I come in again to attack from above the tail, and then turn for another frontal attack, firing from ahead and below the steeply diving Liberator. My aim has never been better. Suddenly there is an explosion, and the blazing crate disintegrates into a shower of wreckage above my head. For a moment I am in danger of collision with falling engines or spinning flaming wings. That would mean certain disaster for me. [...] The falling fuselage of the Liberator misses me by inches as it hurtles into the depths. It falls into the sea some twelve miles south-east of Heligoland.

That was my number five.

[...]

LEFT: A group of German prisoners await interrogation after being captured by a unit of the British 8th Army near the Gargliano River in Italy. 19 January 1944.

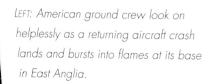

LEFT: American ground crew look on helplessly as a returning aircraft crash lands and bursts into flames at its base in East Anglia.

Dieter [...] keeps hard on the tail of a Fortress, blazing away at it. Tracers from every side converge upon his plane.

He must have become completely insane.

[...] Three thousand feet below, his crate begins emitting a trail of smoke. He opens his canopy, then pushes himself up awkwardly in his seat, and the next moment is thrown clear. His parachute opens. I fly past close to him. His face is contorted with pain, he grips his body. Dieter is wounded.

[...]

At midnight the telephone in my quarters rings.

Lieutenant Dieter Gerhard was found by the crash-boat Falke. He is dead.

[...]

Good night, Dieter. You have earned your rest, after fighting and dying for our beloved German fatherland. You were my best friend: I shall never forget you. Alone now, I shall continue fighting this great battle for Germany, which we both started, you and I together, faithful to the same oath of service which we have sworn.

RIGHT: *An aerial view of the effect of bombs falling from 18 US aircraft on an Italian causeway in 1944.*

BELOW: *An RAF Hudson is refuelled by African workers at a base in West Africa, 1943.*

FRIDAY, 3 SEPTEMBER 1943 – SERGEANT SAM SOLOMON

Having participated in the actions at Gavatu, Tanambago, Guadalcanal and Tulagi Sam writes to a friend.

UNITED STATES MARINE CORPS, PACIFIC THEATRE OF OPERATIONS

We are allowed to say quite a bit now about where we have been and what we have done, […] It's funny, but it wasn't the idea of getting wounded or killed that worried me. Instead, I dreaded the prospect of being caught as the Japs were, with no navy to back them up, no reinforcements and absolutely no chance at all.

152

The time of my big fight came a week or two after we landed on Gavatu, I had dug myself a nice comfortable fox hole which was actually rain proof, mosquito proof, had a candle or two, and even a box to keep chow and water in, in case of attack. It was placed in what I figured was a safe place for a fox hole on the island and was close to our radio dugout. That night, a Sunday night, while on radio watch I copied a coded urgent message from Tulagi. There were forty thousand Jap troops on transports on their way in. Right then our commanding officer figured it was time to send a radio operator to Tanambago. Me!!! That is when that funny feeling hit my knees and the pit of my stomach! I had to leave my nice fox hole and

RIGHT: A British soldier with a Bren gun during the attack on Monte Cassino, Italy.

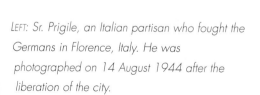

LEFT: Sr. Prigile, an Italian partisan who fought the Germans in Florence, Italy. He was photographed on 14 August 1944 after the liberation of the city.

RIGHT: Men of the Shropshire Yeomanry in northern Italy fire a 5.5" Howitzer, 22 September 1943.

go over where I had none. If I had to fight, I at least wanted a good place to fight from. In case of attack my position was in an old Jap pillbox which stuck up right out in the open like a sore thumb, and would have been blown sky high by a three inch shell. By dawn though, I felt better, for during the night while on guard I heard a rumble and saw flashes of battle way out at sea. And the Jap task force never came in!

[…]

Well, I have work to do, so for now – so long.

YOURS SAM

WEDNESDAY, 26 JANUARY 1944 – TROOP SERGEANT CLIVE BRANSON

Before serving with the Royal Armoured Corps in the Second World War, Branson had fought in the Spanish Civil War with the International Brigade. He was killed a month later during the fighting for the Ngankedank Pass.

BRITISH ARMY, ARAKAN FRONT, BURMA

We are now only a few hundred yards away from glory. 'There are those who would like to philosophise on the question of sacrificing space to save time.' You will remember the reference. But even so, it is still like a mad hatter's picnic. We make our beds down, we sit around and chat, we sunbathe (not so openly as before) and we

RIGHT: GIs of the US 1st Infantry Division board landing craft moored alongside the Esplanade, Weymouth for a pre-D-Day exercise on 1 May 1944.

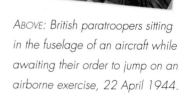

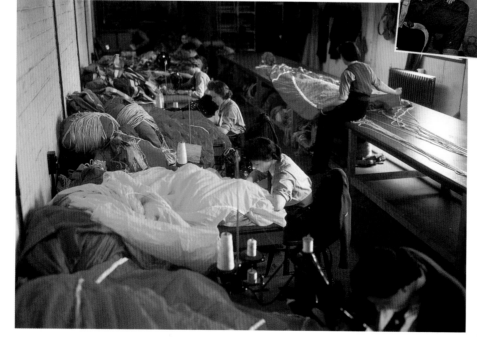

ABOVE: British paratroopers sitting in the fuselage of an aircraft while awaiting their order to jump on an airborne exercise, 22 April 1944.

LEFT: RAF personnel and WAAFs pack parachutes at an RAF base in England, May 1944.

sleep. While overhead scream mortars, etc. To this, and all other incidents of war, such as AA, Jap planes, or our own barrage, the lads react with 'Ignore it' or 'Quiet!', and just carry on sleeping or reading. But I must say one thought runs through my head continually – Spain. This morning a party is going to watch some strategic bombing. I am sending two others of my crew on the principle that the more each man knows of the landscape, the better in every way. The bombers are just coming over. We climbed upon our tanks to have a grandstand view of twelve Liberators and dozens of Vengeance dive-bombers exterminating the Jap position at Razabil cross-roads. Now that the bombers have gone there is a real barrage of small stuff. This may be the solution of the Burma problem. Now I am ever so excited to hear the report of what was the effect. It may seem strange to you that in a sort of way I cannot help gloating over the affair. It is the reverse of Spain a hundredfold.

THURSDAY, 27 APRIL 1944 – L/CPL. HELMUT K.

The letter of Lance Corporal Helmut K. on the retreat from the Crimea, sent via field mail.

GERMAN ARMY, CRIMEA, RUSSIA

My dear parents + Renata,

You are probably worried a great deal about me, waiting impatiently for the mail to arrive every day. But you know, I am writing you as often as I can. I have gone

In order to provide cover for the beach-heads, over 20,000 US and British airborne troops were deployed into Normandy prior to the landings.

LEFT: *General Dwight D Eisenhower, Supreme Commander, Allied Expeditionary Force, chairs a meeting with senior commanders on 1 February 1944 in London.*

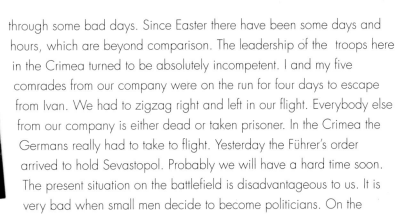

RIGHT: US Marines use flame-throwers to flush out concealed Japanese troops on Bougainville, November 1943.

BELOW: A German soldier killed during the Allied breakthrough at the Giogia Pass, September 1944.

through some bad days. Since Easter there have been some days and hours, which are beyond comparison. The leadership of the troops here in the Crimea turned to be absolutely incompetent. I and my five comrades from our company were on the run for four days to escape from Ivan. We had to zigzag right and left in our flight. Everybody else from our company is either dead or taken prisoner. In the Crimea the Germans really had to take to flight. Yesterday the Führer's order arrived to hold Sevastopol. Probably we will have a hard time soon. The present situation on the battlefield is disadvantageous to us. It is very bad when small men decide to become politicians. On the second day of Easter I received Mother's letter of 28.3.44. So Wernigerode also fell victim to this criminal war! Let's hope that its culprit will soon be put to pillory and convicted. How are you, how are things going? I hope your household will be spared from damage. Now it's only possible to write via airmail. Please give my best regards to all my relatives.

[…]

Giving you my heartiest regards and waiting for your letters,
YOUR HELMUT.

The Battle of Kursk involved two million men, 4,000 aircraft and nearly 6,000 tanks.

FRIDAY, 5 MAY 1944 – SERGEANT SAM SOLOMON

Sam writes again about the horrors of warfare he experienced at Tarawa.

UNITED STATES MARINE CORPS, PACIFIC THEATRE OF OPERATIONS

Dear Mom

Save this picture for me. It shows a group of dead Japs in a hole on Tarawa. The reason that I want it is that I lived right next to this hole for two days and helped bury them by throwing dirt into the hole when the stench became too strong to bear.

Originally there were also a few dead marines in the hole too. We took out the dead marines and covered them with a blanket. Then we threw some more Japs into the hole and covered it over.

The log in the background is in front of a little tunnel which led to another hole. The tunnel too was full of dead marines and Japs.

2 AUGUST 1944 – LT. GEN. TADAMICHI KURIBAYSHI

Whilst facing certain death as the Commander of the Japanese forces on Iwo Jima, General Kuribayshi concerns himself with the safety and happiness of his family in Japan.

LETTER FROM LT GEN TADAMICHI KURIBAYSHI, JAPANESE ARMY, TO HIS WIFE, AUGUST 2, 1944 IWO JIMA

… I hope everyone at home is fine even though we are all in the midst of this big war. Did Tako evacuate to the countryside with her school friends? Did she go to Hiaki alone? I have been concerned about her. I feel sorry that such a little girl like her has to live away from her parents … As far as my well being is concerned, I have endured the inconvenience of life since I came here. Because of my constant awareness of the tides of war, no single day has ever passed without anxiety and tension. It is very likely that our enemy, who plans to invade Saipan and Oomiya Island, will attack us soon in their expedition to invade Japan …

I constantly think about our final destiny here except while I am sleeping. But, I may think about it even in my sleep, for I have had dreams these days …

Although I am not certain about the best place to evacuate around Tokyo, it seems most likely that Tokyo will be subject to daily air-raids within a month or so after our place here is invaded by the enemy. The best place for you to evacuate seems to be

The various battles for Monte Cassino involved major heroics from men of 15 nationalities, including French, Indian, New Zealand, Polish, British and American troops. Great controversy surrounded the Allied bombing of the sixth-century Benedictine abbey which they claimed the Germans were using as part of their defences. In fact, the Germans had already agreed with the Vatican that they would not use it and had kept their word.

RIGHT: Lance Corporal Durrent of Bethnal Green, London rests in the Garigliano River valley on 19 January 1944.

Shinshyu … The war has advanced to the point that we need to think of all these things …

I am sending you my battlefield allowance for the months of June and July. I have heard you would get them after September, though I am not certain if I will still be alive by then …

To my wife. From your husband.

ABOVE: US Marine Corps Corporal Wilbur rests on Guam, 7 January 1944.

PART THREE

TRIUMPH AND DESPAIR

SEVEN

D-DAY

JUNE–DECEMBER 1944

The invasion of Europe was the best-kept and most important secret of the war. The Allies went to enormous lengths to convince the Germans that it would take place somewhere else, on some other date than in Normandy on 6 June 1944. The Germans knew the invasion would happen, but had no idea where and when. Thousands of planners and participants knew most or some of the plans for months, but nothing 'leaked' across the Channel. The Allies even created fictitious armies and landing sites and systematically 'fed' the information to Berlin via double agents. They then intercepted the secret German signals which confirmed that Berlin had 'swallowed' the deception.

A massive bombing campaign preceded the invasion,

BELOW: A lone German soldier looks out to sea alongside an artillery battery forming part of Hitler's Atlantic Wall, 1944.

in which hundreds of French civilians were killed. The French Resistance also played a significant part in undertaking an extensive campaign of sabotage to hinder the German response to the attack. In one significant series of attacks, they managed to delay the journey of the elite SS division *Das Reich* from southern France to Normandy. The journey would normally take three days; sabotage increased it to 17.

Over 23,000 British and American airborne troops began the invasion shortly after midnight, by parachute and glider. Despite much confusion, they managed to secure the flanks of the main beach-heads. The American, British and Canadian ground forces hit the five main landing beaches at dawn. As has been famously portrayed by Steven Spielberg in the remarkable film *Saving Private Ryan*, the Americans encountered a withering hail of fire at Omaha Beach, where casualty rates were as high as 90 per cent in the first wave. But, on the whole, the beach-heads were secured with substantially fewer casualties than the Allies had expected. Allied losses were less than 2,500 on the first day, by the end of which, more than 150,000 men had been put ashore. There were millions of men and mountains of equipment behind them. They would prove to be unstoppable, but the lattice-like hedgerows of the French countryside and astonishing German resistance would take many weeks to wear down.

In the Pacific, there were also significant advances for the Allies. On 15 June a large American force landed on Saipan in the Marianas. There was both a major naval engagement, the Battle of the Philippine Sea, and a ferocious land battle. The Japanese fleet suffered heavy losses, including three aircraft carriers and almost all of their planes. On land, the 30,000 Japanese defenders fought to the death, many as part of mass-suicides, and launched several *Banzai* attacks. The dreadful scenes were later repeated on the islands of Tinian and Guam. Pockets of resistance continued on Guam for the duration of the war. The last Japanese soldier surrendered in 1972.

The capture of these key islands put Tokyo within range of US bombers and led to the resignation of the Japanese Prime Minister, General Tojo. Tinian was ultimately to become the base for the B-29 'Superfortress' bombers that dropped the atom bomb on Hiroshima and Nagasaki.

The Axis Powers were in retreat everywhere. Minsk fell on the Eastern Front. The key city of Falaise in Normandy was taken by the Canadians and a second Allied invasion of France, Operation Dragoon, had taken place in the South of France. Paris liberated itself at the end of August, Brussels was liberated soon after.

The ever-worsening military situation, and Hitler's escalating intransigence in the face of it, gave new impetus to those in the German hierarchy who were plotting to assassinate the *Führer*. The conspiracy began months earlier, but by July 1944 the plotters believed they had enough support to be able to seize power and form an alternative government. The central conspirator, Count Claus von Stauffenberg, planted the bomb, which he'd concealed in his briefcase, only a few feet from Hitler, in his bunker at Rastenburg in East Prussia. By chance, as Stauffenberg rushed to Berlin to initiate the *coup d'état,* the briefcase was inadvertently kicked some distance from Hitler by one of the officers nearby. The bomb exploded, killing four people in the room, but Hitler survived with only minor injuries. Stauffenberg and his fellow conspirators met a grisly end. A moment that could have shortened the war by almost a year, and saved millions of lives, had passed.

Resistance was also growing elsewhere. The second Warsaw rising broke out in August. Forty thousand Poles mounted a take-over of the city despite the fact that only 10 per cent of them had any firearms. They faced overwhelming odds and an apparent reluctance by Stalin to allow the nearby Red Army to help. Nevertheless, they survived for seven weeks. The insurgence got total support from the citizens of Warsaw, despite the mass execution of civilians, which eventually totalled a quarter of the population of the city. The Germans evacuated the entire city after the rising was defeated and later destroyed it as the Soviet tanks advanced.

In October of 1944, the naval battle at Leyte Gulf in the Philippines inflicted another mortal blow on the Japanese military. The Imperial Navy committed almost everything it still had afloat to one last great engagement. The battle was a crushing defeat for Japan, leaving tens of thousands of troops marooned by the American advance. With the fighting fleet decimated and the merchant fleet being gradually destroyed by American submarines, Japan was beaten. Sadly, it would be some time yet before the military leadership would accept reality.

Leyte Gulf saw the appearance of another remarkable example of Japanese fanaticism. The pilots of the 'divine wind' – *Kamikaze* – made their first suicide attacks on the American aircraft carrier *Santee*, killing 16 sailors. *Kamikaze* attacks reached a peak during the invasion of Okinawa six months later. It is thought that over 5,000 pilots died on *Kamikaze* missions during the war.

In Europe, Hitler also threw his last dice in a surprise counter-offensive in the Ardennes, the site of his stunning, disguised onslaught in the Fall of France in 1940. It has become known as the Battle of the Bulge. Hitler committed the best of his soldiers in a lightning attack

to try to reach Antwerp and thus cut the Allied Armies in two. The 'bulge' of the German attack reached 60 miles in depth, before the Allied air forces and their land forces brought the panzers to a halt. The Allies were given an enormous fright, but the Americans, who bore the brunt, responded with great resolve. Yet again, Hitler refused to withdraw and inflicted an even bigger defeat on his army than they would have suffered otherwise, and almost certainly hastened the end of the war.

Hitler's Reich was collapsing everywhere, especially in the east. As the Soviet army approached, countries that had supported the Axis, like Romania, Bulgaria and Hungary, switched sides, but not before their own death squads had settled old scores – in Hungary, they

ABOVE: The end of Hitler's empire was a long and bitter struggle. It was attacked on all sides. Its demise led to the post-war division of Europe, as the Red Army pushed west and the Western Allies pushed east in pursuit of strategic territory.

executed as many remaining Jews as they could find. When the Soviets arrived, a new regime of oppression quickly replaced the one that had just melted away. Even in Greece, a long way from Stalin's 'persuasion', fighting broke out between communists and anti-communists as soon as the Germans were defeated. It was only an emergency intervention from Winston Churchill, on Christmas Day of 1944, that convinced the protagonists to form an all-party government. It was an ominous portent of the post-war world to come.

JUNE–DECEMBER 1944

1944

June 6 Operation Overlord begins with Allied landings in Normandy.

June 12 The D-Day beach-heads are amalgamated.

June 15 The Americans invade Saipan in the Marianas.

June 27 The fall of Cherbourg to the Allies.

July 18 General Tojo resigns as Japanese Prime Minister.

July 20 A bomb plot against Hitler by senior elements of the German army fails.

Aug. 1 The beginning of the second Warsaw rising.

Aug. 15 The Allies land in the South of France.

Aug. 17 Falaise falls to the Allies.

Aug. 23 The rule of dictator Ion Antonescu comes to an end in Romania.

Aug. 25 Paris liberates itself from occupation.

Sep. 3 The British army liberates Brussels.

Sep. 8 The first V2 weapons are launched against Britain.

Sep. 17 An Allied airborne attack is launched in Holland. It proves to be a disaster for the British at Arnhem.

Oct. 2 The second Warsaw rising ends and the city is destroyed by the SS.

Oct. 14 British forces liberate Athens.

Oct. 17 The Americans inflict enormous losses on the Japanese navy in the Battle of Leyte Gulf in the Philippines.

Nov. 7 President Roosevelt wins a fourth term as American President.

Nov. 24 American B29 Superfortress bombing raids on Tokyo begin.

Dec. 16 The German army launches its final counter-offensive of the war in the Ardennes (The Battle of the Bulge).

TUESDAY, 6 JUNE TO SATURDAY, 24 JUNE 1944 – CORPORAL G.E. HUGHES

In this extract from his diary, Hughes details the Allied invasion of Normandy, and the first days of the Battle of Normandy. Sergeant Hughes was hospitalized with malaria for most of the rest of Normandy Campaign.

1ST BATTALION, ROYAL HAMPSHIRE REGIMENT
NORMANDY, FRANCE

6 June 06.00 Get in LCA. Sea very rough. Hit the beach at 7.20 hours. Murderous fire, losses high. I was lucky T[hank] God. Cleared three villages. Terrible fighting and ghastly sights.

7 June Still going. Dug in at 02.00 hrs. Away again at 5.30. NO FOOD. Writing few notes before we go into another village. CO out of action, adjutant killed. P Sgt lost. I do P Sgt['s job]. More later.

8 June 07.30 Fire coming from village. Village cleared. Prisoners taken. Night quite good but German snipers lurking in wood. Had 2 hrs' sleep. Second rest since the 6th.

9 June 06.30 hrs Went on wood clearing. Germans had flown. Only one killed for our morning's work. We are now about 8 to 10 miles inland. Promoted to Sgt.

10 June Joan Darling, I have not had you out of my thoughts. T[hank] God I have come so far. We have lost some good men. Our brigade was only one to gain objectives on D-Day. The French people have given us a good welcome. Had wine.

The main invasion came in 4,000 ships and landing craft, carrying 130,000 ground troops. They were protected by 600 warships.

———

Ten thousand tons of bombs, dropped by 2,500 heavy bombers, preceded the attack, as did a major campaign of disruption by the French Resistance; 7,000 fighter aircraft supported the landings.

———

By the end of June, over 850,000 men had landed in Normandy.

LEFT: German prisoners of war await relocation on a beach compound in Normandy. Prisoners were shipped to permanent camps either in Britain or the US.

166

ABOVE: Prime Minister Winston Churchill, with Field Marshal Sir Alan Brooke (left), visits Commander of the 21st Army Group, General Sir Bernard Montgomery (right), at Monty's mobile HQ in Normandy, 12 June 1944.

11 June Contact with enemy. Lost three of my platoon. Very lucky T[hank] God. Only had 5 hours sleep in 3 days.

12 June This day undescrible [sic] mortar fire and wood fighting. Many casualties. T[hank] God I survived another day.

13 June Just had my first meal since Monday morning. Up all night. Everyone in a terrible state. I keep thinking of u.

14 June Counter-attack by Jerry from woods. Mortar fire. 13 of my platoon killed or missing. After heavy fighting yesterday CSM also wounded, also Joe. O[fficer]

C[ommanding] killed. I am one mass of scratches. Advanced under creeping barrage for 3 miles. Drove Jerry back. It is hell. 3 Tiger tanks came here, up to lines during night.

16 June [resting] Received letter from home. Wrote to Joan and Mum.

17 June [resting]

18 June Day of Hell. Counter-attack.

19 June Day of Hell. Counter-attack

20 June Day of Hell. Advanced. Counter-attack

21 June Quiet day. We have been fighting near Tilley [Tilly]. Bayonet charge. Shelled all day. Letters from home.

22 June Out on patrol. Got within 35 yards of Tiger before spotting it. Got back safely T[hank] God. Shelled to blazes. feeling tired out.

23 June No sleep last night. Exchanged fire, out on patrols all day, went on OP for 4 hours. Stand-to all night. Casualties. Just about had enough.

24 June Had to go back to CCS [Casualty Clearing Station]. Malaria.

TUESDAY, 6 JUNE 1944 – ANNE FRANK

AMSTERDAM, NETHERLANDS

My dearest Kitty,

'This is D-Day,' the BBC announced at twelve. 'This is the day.' The invasion has begun! This morning at eight the British reported heavy bombing of Calais, Boulogne, Le Havre and Cherbourg, as well as Pas de Calais (as usual). Further, as a precautionary measure.for those in the occupied territories, everyone living within a zone of twenty miles from the coast was warned to prepare for bombardment. Where possible, the British will drop pamphlets an hour ahead of time.

According to the German news, British paratroopers have landed on the coast of France. 'British landing craft are engaged in combat with German naval units,' according to the BBC.

Conclusion reached by the Annexe while breakfasting at nine: this is a trial landing, like the one two years ago in Dieppe.

[…]

Oh, Kitty, the best part about the invasion is that I have the feeling that friends are on the way. Those awful Germans have oppressed and threatened us for so long that the thought of friends and salvation means everything to us! Now it's not just the Jews, but Holland and all of occupied Europe. Maybe, Margot says, I can even go back to school in September or October.

YOURS, ANNE M. FRANK

PS. I'll keep you informed of the latest news!

When Count Claus Von Stauffenberg left Hitler's headquarters at Rastenburg and witnessed the bomb blast he had set the fuse for only seconds earlier, he was convinced Hitler was dead because the devastation was so great. He wasn't aware of Hitler's survival until he arrived in Berlin. The conspirators went ahead with their plan anyway.

———

In the subsequent purge, Stauffenberg and at least 5,000 others, including the families of conspirators, were tortured and executed.

ABOVE: *Liberated French children commemorate Bastille Day at the Courselles war memorial.*

FRIDAY, 21 JULY 1944 – ROSEY NORWALK

Rosey, the American Red Cross nurse, arrives in London which is undergoing continual attack from Germany's new 'terror weapons', the V-1. Hitler sanctioned the use of these pilot-less missiles on London in a decision made on 16 May 1944.

JOURNAL, LONDON, ENGLAND

[…] 'We just got a buzz bomb alert.'

Almost in unison we asked what that was. 'It's the Nazi's latest weapon,' he told us, pronouncing it 'Nassi's.' 'A pilotless aircraft – mostly a bomb with wings and motor attached. Looks like a small airplane as it approaches. When the motor cuts off the bomb either falls straight down or explodes or drifts on awhile before falling to explode. You're all right as long as you can hear the motor. Get your helmets back on, girls, as the Nassi's send them over in swarms, any time of the day or night.' And he rushed off to the next compartment.

SEPTEMBER 1944 – PRIVATE IVOR ROWBERY

Private Ivor Rowbery served with the 2nd Battalion, South Staffordshire Regiment attached to the 1st Airborne Division. This farewell letter to his mother was written in September 1944 before the Battle of Arnhem. The letter won first prize in the 1946 Basildon Bond Competition for the Best Letter Written by a Member of the Forces during the Second World War. It was published in the Tatler & Bystander *on 18 September 1946. The magazine introduced it with the following: 'The letter by a Wolverhampton working lad moves me more than some more celebrated literary efforts, and I am grateful to the boy's mother for her permission to reproduce it, because it may help other parents.' Ivor was killed at Arnhem on 17 September 1944.*

The battle for Saipan included the Japanese army's biggest 'Banzai' charge. Usually the last action of a defeated unit, it was a mass charge against the enemy regardless of the hopelessness of the situation. Losses were understandably catastrophic and survivors often committed suicide.

Dear Mom

Usually when I write a letter it is very much overdue, and I make every effort to get it away quickly. This letter, however, is different. It is a letter that I hoped you would never receive, as it is verification of that terse, black-edged card which you received some time ago, and which has caused you so much grief. It is because of this grief that I wrote this letter, and by the time you have finished reading it I hope that it has done some good, and that I have not written it in vain. It is very difficult to write now of future things in the past tense, so I am returning to the present.

To-morrow we go into action. As yet we do not know exactly what our job will be, but no doubt it will be a dangerous one in which many lives will be lost – mine may be one of those lives.

Well, Mom, I am not afraid to die. I like this life, yes – for the past two years I have planned and dreamed and mapped out a perfect future for myself. I would have liked that future to materialise, but it is not what I will but what God wills, and if by sacrificing all this I leave the world slightly better than I found it I am perfectly willing to make that sacrifice. Don't get me wrong though, Mom, I am no flag-waving patriot, nor have I ever professed to be.

England's a great little country (the best there is) but I cannot honestly and sincerely say that it is worth fighting for. Nor can I fancy myself in the role of a gallant crusader fighting for the liberation of Europe. It would be a nice thought but I would only be kidding myself. No, Mom, my little world is centred around you and includes Dad, everyone at home, and my friends at Wolverhampton. That is worth fighting for and if by doing so it strengthens your security and improves your lot in any way, then it is worth dying for too.

Now this is where I come to the point of this letter. As I have already stated, I am not afraid to die and am perfectly willing to do so, if, by my doing so, you benefit in any way whatsoever. If you do not then my sacrifice is all in vain. Have you

ABOVE: Celebrations in Eindhoven, Holland following the town's liberation on 20 September 1944.

ABOVE: A wounded American GI is unloaded from a C-47 transport plane for evacuation to a nearby Army hospital.

RIGHT: US Army Private 1st Class Walter T Stankowski, of the 121st Infantry Regiment of the 8th US Infantry Division, challenges a resident of Dinard, Brittany following its partial destruction by Allied bombers. The resident refused to be evacuated.

benefited, Mom, or have you cried and worried yourself sick? I fear it is the latter. Don't you see Mom, that it will do me no good, and that in addition you are undoing all the good work I have tried to do. Grief is hypocritical, useless and unfair, and does neither you nor me any good.

I want no flowers, no epitaph, no tears. All I want is for you to remember me and feel proud of me, then I shall rest in peace knowing that I have done a good job. Death is nothing final or lasting, if it were there would be no point in living; it is just a stage in everyone's life. To some it comes early, to others late, but it must come to everyone sometime, and surely there is no better way of dying.

Besides I have probably crammed more enjoyment into my 21 years than some manage to do in 80. My only regret is that I have not done as much for you as I would have liked to do. I loved you, Mom, you were the best Mother in the World, and what I failed to do in life I am trying to make up for in death, so please don't let me down, Mom, don't worry or fret, but smile, be proud and satisfied. I never had much money, but what little I have is all yours. Please don't be silly and sentimental about it, and don't try to spend it on me. Spend it on yourself or the kiddies, it will do some good that way. Remember that where I am I am quite O.K., and providing I know that you are not grieving over me I shall be perfectly happy.

Well Mom, that is all, and I hope I have not written it all in vain.

Goodbye, and thanks for everything.

Your unworthy son, IVOR

One of the worst V weapon attacks on Britain hit the Guards Chapel at Wellington Barracks during a service, killing 121 people.

172

SUNDAY, 10 SEPTEMBER 1944 – ROSEY NORWALK

Rosey, mindful of the strict security blanket still in operation, limited her filming to days out in the country and up to London.

JOURNAL, SOUTHAMPTON, ENGLAND

If only I could take movies of the armies moving through this port. That's a lost cause, of course – the films would be destroyed and I'd probably be sent home in disgrace. But what sights we see each day, things I'll never forget.

BELOW: A landing ship dock (LSD) on course for Morotai as part of the invasion flotilla, 14 September 1944. The invasion took place the following day.

MONDAY, 16 OCTOBER 1944 – LESLIE R. PETERSON

The following description of a typical mission of a B-17 in the 457th Bomb Group of the 8th Air Force was excerpted from a letter written by Leslie R. Peterson to his wife on 16 October 1944. The letter was only recently found among some family memorabilia.

ENGLAND

Dear Mildred,

Well, tonight comes the story of a mission. […]

Now it is time to start the bomb run. For the next 15 or 20 minutes, we are working for the government. Right straight down flak alley, not changing our course, altitude or moving out of formation. We are up about five miles now, and the next plane is about ten feet off our wing. I'm on the inter-phone now with a special job to do that I can't write about. I have to watch the seconds tick by on my watch and they seem like hours. Suddenly over the inter-phone, 'Flak! 12 o'clock level.' And here it comes; we'll be pounded for the next eight to ten minutes. I can feel it now bouncing the ship around as it hits close. I can hear it rattle off the ship quite often, too. There's a sharp sucking sound, a sharp crack, then a dull boom like a heavy door slamming. That was a 38mm and it burst right above the wing. I glance up through the hatch, see a

173

ABOVE: GIs pose with letters from home on a European beachhead.

RIGHT: 8 July 1944. US Marines on Saipan.

LEFT: As 1944 drew to a close American losses in the Pacific were continuing to escalate as Japanese determination grew. Dedication ceremony of the 'Farewell to Thee' memorial in honour of the Pearl Harbor victims.

puff of black smoke and feel the ship jump. Right in front of an engine, there is another burst. Bob (Sonday, tailgunner) yells out, 'B-17 going down in flames!' There it is, 'chutes piling out; what a sickening sight to see one of these wonderful planes sliding down out of control.

'Bomb bay doors open,' calls the bombardier. Whoosh, bang, that flak is pretty

accurate. We keep bouncing around; luckily no one gets hit. 'Bombs away,' calls the bombardier. I open the radio room door and check. Sure enough, all bombs are dropped. What a blessed relief; we can evade some of that stuff now. In a minute or two, we are out of the flak and get a chance to look around. Look at that cloud of flak we just came through; there's a regular lane of it with still more planes coming through it.

Now we watch out for fighters, but usually they don't bother us after the bomb run. Another hour or two and we are over friendly territory […]

LEFT: An F6F Hellcat fighter aborts its landing run at sunset on the USS Randolph aircraft carrier. It passes over the silhouette of the ship's 40mm anti-aircraft guns.

Thursday, 20 July 1944 – Theodor Morell, Hitler's personal physician

At 12.42pm a bomb, placed under a table in the map room of the Führer's Headquarters at Rastenburg in East Prussia, exploded. Hitler received relatively superficial injuries, as detailed by his physician below, and he was able to meet with Mussolini as planned later in the afternoon. Lt. Col. Claus Schenck Graf von Stauffenberg who planted the bomb and three co-conspirators are executed at around 11.00pm that night. Shortly after midnight Hitler speaks to the German people on radio stating that he perceives his survival 'as a confirmation of my assignment from Providence to carry on my life's goal as I have done hitherto'.

RASTENBURG, EAST PRUSSIA

[Morning] Patient A: administered eye drops, conjunctivitis in right eye.

[After the explosion] One-fifteen p.m.: pulse 72. Eight p.m. pulse 100, regular, strong, blood pressure 165–70.

Treated injuries with penicillin powder.

Right forearm badly swollen, prescribed acid aluminium acetate compress. Effusion of blood on right shinbone has subsided. On back of third and fourth finger of left hand there is a large blister. Bandage. Occiput partly and hair completely singed, a palm-sized second-degree burn on the middle of the calf and a number of contusions and open flesh wounds. Left forearm has effusion of blood on interior aspects and is badly swollen; he can move it only with difficulty. He is to take Optalidons at once, and two tablespoons of Brom-Nervacit before going to sleep.

Friday, 21 July 1944 – Anne Frank

By now Anne Frank had been hiding with her family in an Amsterdam attic for over two years. Optimistically she looked for liberation before the start of school again in the autumn. Her dreams were not to be realized. Arrested by the Gestapo on 4 August 1944 she was eventually moved to Bergen-Belsen Concentration Camp. She died there in late February or early March 1945 of typhus, along with 25,000 others in those months. The camp was liberated by British troops on 15 April 1945.

AMSTERDAM, NETHERLANDS

Dearest Kitty,

I'm finally getting optimistic. Now, at last, things are going well! They really are! Great News! An assassination attempt has been made on Hitler's life, and for once not by Jewish Communists or British capitalists, but by a German general who's not only a count, but young as well. The Führer owes his life to 'Divine Providence': he escaped, unfortunately, with only a few minor burns and scratches. A number of

---

Churchill and Roosevelt had little to bargain with at Yalta. The Red Army had amassed more than 180 divisions in the defeat of Germany and controlled an empire from Berlin to the Pacific.

officers and Generals who were nearby were killed or wounded. The head of the conspiracy has been shot.

This is the best proof we've had so far that many officers and generals are fed up with the war and would like to see Hitler sink into a bottomless pit, so they can establish a military dictatorship, make peace with the Allies, rearm themselves and, after a few decades, start a new war. Perhaps Providence is deliberately biding its time getting rid of Hitler, since it's much easier, and cheaper, for the Allies to let the impeccable Germans kill each other off. It's less work for the Russians and British, and it allows them to start rebuilding their own cities that much sooner. But we haven't reached that point yet, and I'd hate to anticipate the glorious event.
[…]

YOURS, ANNE M. FRANK

After the liberation of Auschwitz, the Soviet authorities announced that four million people had died there. The figure was revised after the fall of communism to 1.1 million, 1 million of whom were Jews.

THURSDAY, 3 AUGUST 1944 – THE UNKNOWN BROTHER AND SISTER OF LODZ GHETTO

This diary was discovered by a returning Polish Jew after the liberation of Lodz by the Soviet Army. It was written in the margins of a discarded French novel by an unknown teenage boy. The diary was written in four languages.

LODZ, POLAND

When I look on my little sister my heart is melting. Hasn't the child suffered its part? She has fought so heroically the last five years. When I look on our cosy little room tidied up by the young intelligent poor being I am getting saddened by the thought that soon she will have to leave our last particle of home.

Oh God in heaven, why didst thou create Germans to destroy humanity? I don't even know if I shall be allowed to be together with my sister. I cannot write more. I am resigned terribly and black spirited.

FRIDAY, 15 SEPTEMBER 1944 – THEODOR MORELL

RASTENBURG, EAST PRUSSIA

Patient A[dolf Hitler] shows increasing signs of stress as recorded in the personal diary of his physician. The following day Hitler, in a directive, demanded 'fanatical determination' from 'every able-bodied man … all we can do is hold our positions or die. Officers … are responsible for kindling this fanaticism in the troops and in the general population'.

Patient A, at six p.m. Blood pressure 150mm, heart tones pure and regular, 84 beats per minute. Pulse good and full. Complaints of dizziness, throbbing head, and return of the tremor to his legs, particularly the left, and hands.

A lot of worries!

Left ankle swollen, particularly on left shinbone above the ankle. Some time ago there was an eczema on the shinbone which vanished because of Mutaflor cure.

I recommended: adequate oxygen intake either by a eight- or ten- day stay at Berghof or by going for drives in an open car every other day, with or without interrupting the drive for half an hour's walk. Also massage to improve the blood supply and treat the swollen left foot and ankle.

Brom-Nervacit causing it. Is this possible?

As it contains saccharin and yeast, yes. Fermentation of the sugar.

I ought to have it chemically analysed.

Should try to put his left leg up as often as possible.

Only perform the really vital functions himself. Shed as much load as possible.

SIGNED) PROFESSOR MORELL.

FRIDAY, 29 SEPTEMBER 1944 – GEORGE LEINSTER

George Leinster was a captain in the Sherwood Rangers Yeomanry. After service in North Africa, he took part in the Normandy campaign. This letter is a first-hand account of the British Liberation Army's advance through France, Belgium and Holland.

CAPT. G. S. T. LEINSTER, SHERWOOD RANGERS YEOMANRY, B. L. A.
FRIDAY 29TH SEPTEMBER 1944

My Dearest Mother,

If I am to write you the long letter I have been promising for several weeks, it must be type-written, so please excuse that.

[…]

My failure to write earlier has not been due to being always on the move. Between our periods of movement and excitement we have been able to have short but very pleasant rests. These 'rests' are often my busiest times, and somehow I always just failed to write the fuller type of letter. Often too, experiences crowded on one another so fast that there was too much to say in anything less than a small book. Now that another phase seems to have ended, it is possible to look back and see things in truer perspective.

On that and on many other occasions we have felt that if the Germans were not such swines we could feel some pity for them. We feel not a shred of pity. I have talked with many German prisoners; I do not do so now as they make me feel furious. They have a sort of mental leprosy which render parts of their minds and emotions entirely insensitive. I know that when they are destroying and burning in their heyday they felt no pang or qualm for the suffering they caused. That they lack a sense of personal conscience is understandable, but it is baffling to find all their kinder emotions equally atrophied.

> The exact number of dead in the Dresden firestorm will never be known. The heat was so intense, an unknown number of bodies were obliterated. The simple inscription on the mass grave in Dresden's cemetery reads: 'How many dead?'

How you who have not come into close contact with the Germans can hope to understand them I do not know. It is difficult enough for us who meet them constantly. I hope that those who control our post-war relations with Germany shall be men who know the German as the Soldier does. [...]

The Germans were very frightened of the Maquis, the armed civilians, in France and Belgium. It was the fear of a guilty conscience. They were delighted to surrender to us and so be protected against the vengeance of the partisans. Never was protection given less willingly. There were many cases in which natural justice was speedily meted out by the civilians. We could not countenance this when we were present, but did not regret it when we could not prevent it.

The joy of the people is equalled only by their hatred of the Germans. This can almost be felt. Their great fear is that the mass of the English, so far away in detached England, will again be too lenient towards the Germans owing to a mistaken sense of fair play. Most of them wish to see the Germans literally exterminated, and all say we must go right to Berlin and impose our will from there. We realise how fortunate we are that England is an island; it is hard for Englishmen to appreciate the feelings of these smaller countries who are on Germany's doorstep and who cannot stand up to Germany without strong support. I think our prestige has been very high since Autumn 1940, when we stood alone, but never in all our history has it been so high, at least in Europe, as it is today.

[...]

It was strange to [...] see the huge cemeteries of the last war, stretching away over the plains with their limitless rows of small white crosses, the imagination boggling over so much slaughter. None of this war's cemeteries, not even that at Al Alamein, compare in size with these we saw, and I still think that this is an easy war for the soldier in every way in comparison with that of 1914–1918.

[...]

Mail is arriving faster than ever from home just now. We have been receiving English papers the day after they are published, and have plenty to read though not much time to do it in. The cigarettes and tobacco were very welcome. If you are sending any more, please make it cigarettes only, as my tobacco stock is high just now. We left the Normandy area with piles of cigarettes, chocolate and sweets, but over some hundreds of miles these have been given away until now we can only give away some of up our issue cigarettes and chocolate. I wish we could have given away a hundred times as much. All these people had only a few rationed, foul cigarettes and had not seen chocolate for more than 4 years. How pleased they are when we give them a bar! They give us all they can, we give them all we can, there is no mention of money at all, and it is all quite a Christian affair. For four months now, money has just not meant a thing to me; I rather like it.

RIGHT: An American female Red Cross volunteer enjoys a picnic at Mindoro in the liberated Philippine Islands.

I must close. Take care of yourself – I should be back in a few months to tell you all the stories.

My love, Dear Mother, as Ever to All.

XXX GEORGE XXX'

MONDAY, 6 NOVEMBER 1944 – ROSEY NORWALK

Rosey, ever mindful of the on-going censorship of letters, records items such as this in her personal journal. She was writing about Private Paul S. Shimer Jr. of Chambersburg, Pennsylvania. The ceremony took place on 25 October 1944. He is mentioned again in her diary on 27 January 1945.

JOURNAL, SOUTHAMPTON, ENGLAND

Before I collapse for the night should note that the ceremony I was hinting about to the family [in a letter written the same day] was a celebration of the loading of the Millionth Yank to go through this Port. A nice-looking private from Pennsylvania, the poor guy was overwhelmed with all the brass making a fuss over him and hanging a big sign around his neck. He's one of the many infantry replacements going over these days. Sure hope he makes it through, as we're hearing how much tougher the fighting is getting these past few weeks. Our work schedule is often around the clock as thousands of replacement troops are loading through here.

When British forces freed the inmates at Belsen concentration camp, they found 30,000 emaciated people still alive and 35,000 unburied bodies. Despite all medical help, 300 people a day for several days continued to die after liberation.

EIGHT

GÖTTERDÄMMERUNG

JANUARY-JULY 1945

As 1945 dawned in Europe, the twilight of Hitler's Reich was advancing with ever-increasing speed, despite amazingly stubborn defence by the German army. They were heavily outnumbered on the Eastern Front, and even the highly mobile panzers could not move quickly enough to defend new Soviet breakthroughs.

On 27 January the Red Army liberated Auschwitz. But the Nazis had not finished with the Jews. Many who had survived the camps were either shot as the Soviets approached, or were forced to march west towards Germany. The marches were at least as bad, if not worse than the camps. The prisoners were extremely weak, had no food and no winter clothing. Thousands died on the roads, thousands more died when they reached the camps in Germany.

The city of Dresden had so far escaped Allied bombing; its historic buildings were still intact. But, following a Soviet request for air support to prevent German reinforcements reaching the Eastern Front in Silesia, the Allies chose to attack the marshalling yards at Dresden. The bombing itself was intense, but a firestorm started which consumed eleven square miles of the city. The fires burned for a week. The death toll was at least 60,000.

As the killing continued unabated, the Allies were planning the new world order that would follow the war. The victors would have what was due to them. Territorially there was little room for negotiation: the Big Three would control what their armies held. There was little Roosevelt or Churchill could do about the new Soviet sphere of influence which would result from the gains of the Red Army. Stalin had millions of battle-hardened soldiers who had managed to humble the mighty *Wehrmacht*. 'Big Three' co-operation, as expressed at these major wartime meetings at Teheran, Yalta and finally Potsdam, were co-operative only as far as the existence of war demanded. There was no ideological common ground and plenty of territory to be argued over. All three leaders had to have one eye on the war, and one on the strategic carve-up of the post-war world.

On both the Eastern and Western Fronts, every square mile of territory won or lost cost hundreds of German and Allied lives. It was bitter, often street-by-street, hand-to-hand fighting. Allied advances often trapped tens of thousands of German prisoners. But still, the Germans constantly regrouped and prepared yet another redoubt. The army consistently responded to Hitler's implorings for more and more sacrifice, despite the losses among their colleagues and among their loved ones in the decimated German cities. The predominant psychology is difficult to comprehend. Was it frightened desperation, or vainglorious belief in the survival of the Reich, or a perverse combination of both? Certainly, the Allied demand for unconditional surrender, announced by Roosevelt at the Casablanca conference in 1943, stiffened German resistance. It also meant that Germany would ultimately become a post-war political vacuum that the Allies would readily fill and create the future partition of Europe that would become the progenitor for the Cold War.

RIGHT: As the Allies continued to push into German occupied Europe, troops were able to be relieved. This photograph was described officially as being of the first British soldier to come home on leave, Private G Thomas. He arrived in London on New Year's day, 1945.

However, by April the *Wehrmacht*, save those who would fight to the end to protect Hitler in his bunker in Berlin, had finally fallen apart. The raised hands of surrender were now more common than the clenched fists of defiance. Sadly for the Allies, April was also the month of the loss of one of their leaders. Roosevelt and Churchill had become the cornerstones of the western

Allies, but on 12 April 1945, Roosevelt collapsed from a cerebral haemorrhage and died within a couple of hours. His health had declined rapidly, but his weakness had been kept from the public and his death came as a huge shock in America and elsewhere. As the burden of responsibility for conducting the war shifted, day by day, to America's shoulders, Roosevelt's stature grew.

He died during his fourth term as president and will be remembered as one of its greatest leaders.

His successor, Harry Truman, had a tough act to follow. He had been vice-president for only three months, and although the war was all but over, he would soon face one of the most difficult decisions ever to confront a world leader. He hadn't known about the Manhattan Project until he was sworn in as president. The decision to form a scientific committee to study whether it was possible to make a nuclear weapon was taken by Roosevelt as early as 1939, when Albert Einstein had written to him to alert him to the possibility that not only could it be done, but that Germany might have a head start. When the scientists agreed that it was possible, Roosevelt approved a two billion dollar programme that occupied 600,000 people for four years to construct the new weapon. It would be Truman's decision to use it. It would bring about the end of the war and shape global politics for at least the rest of the century.

The last days of the Reich became a macabre drama of liberation and death. In each village and town the liberating armies found new horror stories. The Nazis hurried to find old enemies, still alive in the camps, so that scores could finally be settled. They started executing one another, using any variant on the theme of 'defeatism' as an excuse. By now, Hitler was recruiting boys and old men to the cause in Berlin. At the same time, 30 generals and 300,000 men were surrendering to the Allies in the Ruhr.

Finally, even the rats left the sinking ship. Heinrich Himmler tried to open negotiations with the Allies in a plan to join forces to fight the Soviets. Hermann Göring fled to Berchtesgaden and offered himself as Hitler's successor. Hitler was furious, but they were out of his reach. His old ally, Benito Mussolini, didn't enjoy the protection of his personal entourage. His end came ignominiously in a summary execution and a public display and humiliation of his corpse. The following day, the entire German army in Italy surrendered.

When the end came in Germany, it produced scenes at least as terrible as all the other horrors of the war. The death of Hitler was a brief prelude. Hitler had married Eva Braun on 29 April. The next day they retired to their private quarters where Braun took poison and Hitler shot himself. The bodies were burned in a shell hole outside the bunker where the remains were discovered by the Red Army. It was a sordid end.

What ensued on the streets of Berlin was akin to pursuing animals in a trap. The SS shot anyone who wouldn't fight. They rounded up civilians and made them fight under threat of death. It became an orgy of killing. The Red Army lost 300,000 men in the battle for the city, its highest casualty rate of the war. The Germans lost close to 200,000 soldiers and more than 100,000 civilians. The murder, rape and looting which had characterized the German advance eastwards had been returned in equal measure by the Soviet advance westwards. In Berlin, the very depths of brutality were plumbed.

Berlin fell on 2 May. The formal surrender came six days later. The Thousand Year Reich was no more. Up to the moment of his death, Hitler still raged about his enemies and how the Jews had destroyed his dreams. He had systematically murdered six million Jews in a policy of genocide which has no parallel anywhere in history. The death toll in the extermination camps was appalling. 400,000 died in Chelmo, Poland; 300,000 in Sobibor, Poland; 600,000 in Belzec; and at least 700,000 in Treblinka. Of the 6,000,000 Jews estimated to have been murdered during the Second World War, 3 million were Polish and 1 million were Russian. German Jewish losses were 160,000, fewer than in many countries of German conquest such as Czechoslovakia, Hungary and Romania. Fortunately for the world, it was not the end of a great culture; of a people with an amazing historical legacy. But it was a massacre of innocents that will live forever as the ultimate example of evil.

JANUARY–JULY 1945

1945

Jan. 17 The Soviet army liberates Warsaw.

Jan. 18 The German garrison in Budapest surrenders to the Soviets.

Jan. 27 The advancing Red Army liberates Auschwitz.

Feb. 4 Roosevelt, Stalin and Churchill meet at Yalta in the Soviet Crimea. The division of Germany and Korea is agreed, as is the first conference on the formation of a United Nations.

Feb. 13 Sixty thousand people are thought to have been killed by the Allied bombing of Dresden.

Mar. 7 The first Allied troops cross the Rhine at Remagen.

Mar. 23 American troops break out from their bridgeheads on the Rhine.

Mar. 29 The Red Army enters Austria.

Apr. 11 The American army reaches the river Elbe, 75 miles from Berlin.

Apr. 12 President Roosevelt dies and is succeeded by his Vice-President Harry S. Truman.

Apr. 25 American and Soviet troops meet at Leckwitz and at Torgau on the river Elbe.

Apr. 25 Fifty-one countries sign the UN Charter at its founding conference in San Francisco.

Apr. 28 Benito Mussolini and his entourage, including his mistress, Clara Petacci, are shot by partisans. Their bodies are strung up for display in Milan the next day.

Apr. 29 The German army surrenders on the Italian Front.

Apr. 30 After marrying Eva Braun the day before, Hitler commits suicide in his bunker in Berlin.

May 2 Berlin surrenders to the Red Army.

May 8 Following the formal surrender of Germany the day before, 'Victory in Europe' (VE) day is declared.

July 26 Churchill loses the British General election to a Labour Party landslide. Clement Attlee becomes the new Prime Minister.

Saturday, 27 January 1945 – Rosey Norwalk

Rosey described in her journal the departure of Private Shimer from Southampton for France. One million GIs and only three months later she makes this entry.

Journal, Southampton, England

Realized I forgot to note that the 2,000,000th Yank embarked from this Port on the sixteenth, with appropriate ceremonies. Similar to those held for the 1,000,000th Yank whose departure we celebrated last October, that shy young private from Pennsylvania. I still see him standing halfway up the gangway, very embarrassed as the British and American brass singled him out and presented him with a new mess kit, hanging that 1,000,000th Yank cardboard sign around his neck. We just heard that he was killed six weeks after he landed in France. I sure hope this guy has better luck.

Sunday, 28 January 1945 – Lev Kopelev

Lev Kopelev's description of the situation in Allenstein, East Prussia, after its capture by Soviet troops in late January 1945.

Russian Army, Allenstein, East Prussia

[...] the city is corrupting soldiers: trophies, women, drinking. We were told that the division commander, Colonel Smirnov, had personally shot a Lieutenant, who had

organized his soldiers to stand in line to rape a German woman lying in a gateway.

At the headquarters we heard about another recent terrible incident. Several Russian girls, who had been deported to Germany, worked as waitresses in our headquarters casino. Being civilians, they did not wear uniforms, but they were lavishly supplied with captured clothes. One of them [...] had been the most beautiful among them, young, well built, cheerful, she had been wearing her golden hair in waves falling to her shoulders, the way German and Polish women do. [...] Yesterday she was carrying a bucket of soup

RIGHT: The Yalta Conference, 4 February 1945: US President Roosevelt is flanked by Churchill and Stalin. The Conference determined the post-war demarcation of Germany between the Allied Powers.

LEFT: New Year's Eve 1944: USAAF Pilot Dick Perley poses with the accumulated alcohol ration for a unit party at Toul-Ochey, France.

INSET RIGHT: A wounded American GI sits with a wounded German prisoner of war at an American First Aid Post.

across the street. Several drunken soldiers were wandering around. They saw her: 'Hey-ho, German bitch!' – and a burst from a submachine gun hit her in the back. She died on the spot, crying, saying 'Why, what for...?'

[...]

Marshal Rokossovsky's order was read aloud at the headquarters: robbery, rape, theft, murder of civilians should be punished by death on the spot according to martial law.

ABOVE: Nuremberg, Germany, 1945. The once proud site for Hitler's parades is devastated by Allied bombing. This picture was taken after its occupation by Allied troops.

LEFT: Germany. As the Allies push closer to the heart of the Reich small pockets of resistance are encountered. Here, members of Company F of the US 325th Glider Infantry Regiment use phosphor grenades to clear their path of advance.

WEDNESDAY, 21 MARCH 1945 – CORPORAL LESLIE LIEBER

As the Allied armies pushed deeper into Germany a military government was installed into the occupied zones to resurrect law and order and bring back a sense of normality to the German people.

AMERICAN MILITARY GOVERNMENT, US ZONE OF OCCUPATION, GERMANY

For the last two mornings I have been interpreting and gradually handling more and more problems of civilians at the Military Government office. They are swamped with work, and there are hundreds of people lined up at the door every morning. I am very happy to be able to get acquainted with what's on the Germans' minds, how they act and feel. In two days I have spoken to about a hundred. They are almost invariably old people, or past military age.

Many Germans have been hired to work as stenographers and interpreters, and they seem to enjoy their work. Everyone knows there are Nazis amongst them, but no one seems to care, because they are not in a position, because of the nature of their jobs, to do any harm to the allied cause – and in cases where their talents are needed, they are put to work. This causes consternation in people who claim to have hated Nazism (of whom there will soon be 65,000,000) in this country!

Two women who have helped the Allies by denouncing outstanding Nazis around here came in this morning, and casting a side glance next to them, whispered to me, 'What's that Nazi, Herr –, doing here?' I asked a couple of our officers and they said not to worry – the place is full of them.

So far, I have not seen a scowl cross a German's face. Sometimes our treatment of them is mild and considerate, sometimes rough and tough. The reaction of the Germans under the two extremes of treatment is exactly the same. You can yell at them, bark at them, treat them like dogs, and they don't bat an eyelash. That intuitive knowledge one has sometimes of what must be flitting through the mind of a person, even though he succeeds pretty well in masking his face, doesn't apply here. The German doesn't seem to resent being lambasted at all. He displays no emotion and returns a civil answer. He seems to be completely cowed by the sheepish policy of the follow-the-leader practised for so long in this country. For one thing, they were all primed to being cut up and quartered like so many ribs of beef – by German propaganda warning them of our coming. They seem pleasantly surprised at being alive and seem to feel that a little bellowing on our part is the ???

[…]

Today a man, who looked as if he could never smile again, walked in with a dazed-looking boy who seemed to be seeing the world for the first time. He said his wife was Jewish and his four children half Jewish he had hidden them, more or less, for the last four years in something resembling a stable. For the last year, the most

Benito Mussolini tried to avoid capture by dressing in a German uniform and escaping to Switzerland, but he was recognized.

terrible conditions prevailed, because of the Gestapo, so that they had to disappear from the face of the earth, to all intents and purposes. All six had to live on his Aryan food and clothing card and whatever else a desperate husband in those circumstances could scrounge. They have all been sleeping and sitting on the floor for four years – that is, when they weren't standing up. What he wanted was a couple of beds and chairs. Like all cases having nothing to do with military or general food and health questions, he was told to make these requests of the Burgermeister, who has been instructed to see that all civilians have sufficient food and lodgings.[…]

SUNDAY, 15 APRIL 1945 – DIETER BORKOWSKI

An entry from the diary of Dieter Borkowski, a 16-year-old flight assistant, on the mood of the Berlin population during the last days of the Reich. Borkowski was forced to participate in the battle for Berlin, was taken prisoner and released by the Soviets in the late summer of 1945.

GERMAN VOLKSSTURM, GRIMMSTRASSE 17
APRIL 15, 1945.
… At noon we left the Anhalt Station in a completely crowded suburban train. There

BELOW: As the Reich collapsed the debris of battle was strewn in every town and city as the Allied armies advanced on the capital.

RIGHT: *Buchenwald was liberated by the US 80th Infantry Division on 11 April 1945. The true horror of the Final Solution was revealed.*

BELOW: *Even after liberation many thousands were so malnourished that survival was nearly impossible.*

were a lot of women on the train – refugees from the eastern parts of Berlin, already captured by Russians. They were carrying all their belongings with them – a tightly packed backpack, and that was all. Their faces frozen from fear, people were angry and desperate! I have never heard people cursing so bitterly. …

Suddenly somebody shouted through the noise: 'Silence!' We saw a plain-looking dirty soldier, with two Iron Crosses and a golden German Cross on his uniform. He had a badge on his sleeve with four small metal tanks, which meant that he had destroyed 4 tanks in close combat. 'I want to tell you something' – he shouted, and the whole carriage fell silent – 'Even if you do not want to listen! Stop whining! We have to win this war, we should not lose our courage. If the others win – the Russians, the Poles, the French, the Czechs – and if they will do to our people just one percent of what we have been doing to them for six years, there will be not a single German left alive in several weeks. I know what I am talking about, I have spent six years in the occupied countries!' It was so quiet in the train, that one could have heard if a pin drop.

MONDAY, 23 APRIL 1945 – GENERAL DER FLIEGER KARL KOLLER

Koller was Luftwaffe Chief of General Staff and was in close contact with events in the last days of the Reich. The suspicion that Goebbels' children would be killed proved correct: Magda Goebbels poisoned their six children and then killed herself. Goebbels shot himself. The bodies of Dr Goebbels and his wife were then removed from the bunker, doused in petrol and set alight. When the bunker was finally captured by Soviet troops their charred and distorted remains were discovered on ground nearby.

190

BERLIN, GERMANY

After having previously informed me by telephone from the bunker that events of historical importance were taking place and that he had something important to tell me, Christian reached me at 2045 hours and reported verbally:

'The Führer had had a breakdown, considers continuation of the war hopeless, does not want to leave Berlin, wants to remain in the bunker and accept the consequences. [...] all his documents and papers [were] brought into the courtyard from the bunker and burnt there. He ordered Goebbels to come and his wife and children are all sitting there with him now, in the bunker.'

When I asked what was going to happen to them, Christian answered: 'They will probably kill the children and the adults will commit suicide.'

[...] The atmosphere in the bunker has affected me deeply. An impression I cannot begin to explain.'

ABOVE: Units of the US and Soviet armies met on 25 April 1945 at Torgau on the River Elbe.

BELOW: Benito Mussolini and his mistress, Clara Petacci, were captured by Italian Partisans and executed on 28 April 1945.

TUESDAY, 1 MAY 1945 – JOHN RABE

John Rabe had been head of Siemens in Nanking during the Japanese attack. Recalled to Germany in 1938, he worked throughout the war as a clerk at the Siemens plant in the Berlin district constructed by the Company. He took up his diary again as the capital of the 1,000 year Reich was about to be captured. To avoid capture and humiliation, Hitler and his by then wife, Eva Braun, had committed suicide on 30 April by swallowing poison. Hitler also shoots himself through the mouth.

SIEMENSSTADT, BERLIN, GERMANY

Our most recent billeted soldiers, a Russian noncom [medical student] and several privates, had to move on yesterday, much to our regret. They were relatively decent fellows [relatively inserted as an after thought], who gave us some of their rations now and then. No sooner were they gone than three Russian soldiers forced their way in, looking for girls.

TOP: *German prisoners of war in Bolzano, May 1945. A rapid process of de-Nazification and screening began as soon as prisoners were taken.*

ABOVE: *Civilians take their few possessions through the rubble of buildings that Nazi architect Albert Speer had designed.*

[…]

A seventeen-year-old girl was raped five times, then shot. The women in a bomb shelter on Quell Weg were raped while their husbands looked on. Herr Gabbert was stopped on the street and had to take off most of his clothes because he claimed he had no jewelry. A ring he had hidden in his shoe was then taken. Only a little shelling overnight, but heavier this morning. Himmler has shot himself, or so the Russians say. [Russian rumours proved to be wrong – Himmler was arrested by the British on 24 May.] On 28 April the Anglo-American forces were about 20 miles outside of Munich, which they have probably taken by now. These are just oral reports from Russian soldiers.

[…]

5 p.m. I've just come from a walk that I took with Willi through Seimnsstadt to see if we could scare up some food of any kind somewhere. No success. There's nothing more to be had.

[…]

We're told that a German-speaking Russian staff officer is living at 43 Rohr Damm, to whom you can apply for help if you're molested by Russian soldiers. They say the same officer is in charge of getting supplies to the civilian population promptly. That sounds very promising.

LEFT: An American 105mm self-propelled gun fires at sunset.

WEDNESDAY, 9 MAY 1945 – TAMARAH LAZERSON

Tamarah was a 13-year-old Lithuanian girl who lived in Kovno and was then sent to a ghetto. Her parents were killed and Tamarah went on to finish her studies in Chemistry and married fellow student Michael Ostrowsky.

KOVNO

Yesterday Germany surrendered unconditionally. The war is over. Red flags fly triumphantly over Kovno. At long last the ugly Fascists have been decisively defeated … Whatever may come, I am delighted that the dictator had been brought to his knees. The arrogant fiend who touted 'Germany, Germany above all' now has to stoop to the barbarian of the East – the USSR.

ABOVE: The wreckage of a downed Japanese bomber in the Pacific.

LEFT: The American aircraft carrier USS Franklin *arrives on 19 March 1945 at the Brooklyn Navy Yard after sustaining massive damage in Japanese kamikaze attacks in the Pacific Ocean.*

ABOVE: British Field-Marshal Montgomery and Soviet Marshal Zhukov walk along the Unter den Linden in Berlin on 12 July 1945.

RIGHT: VE Day – London, 8 May 1945. A small girl who has yet to live in or know a world at peace.

You have lost; just as proud and mighty Rome did not rise out of its ashes, so Germany will not raise her head again above the nations of the world. She has fallen. Her strong might has been crushed forever. Long live peace! Honour to the heroes who raised the flag of victory over the contemptible towers of Berlin.

NINE

VICTORY IN THE PACIFIC

JANUARY–SEPTEMBER 1945

The brutality, human degradation and death which characterized the end of the war in Europe, was replicated in the final months of the war in the Pacific. Just as in Europe, hostility turned into hatred, atrocities evoked vengeance. In the final days it became an orgy of bloodletting.

The first major objective of the year, in the Americans' relentless determination to reach Japan, was Manila, capital of the Philippines. The Americans reached the outskirts of the city at the beginning of February 1945, but it took a month to take the city. The Japanese defenders numbered a quarter of a million. The fighting was fierce; the city was severely damaged in the course of the action. Many of the Japanese defenders

BELOW: A USMC flame-throwing tank destroys captured Japanese aircraft near Sasebo, Japan. 2 November 1945. The Allies were fearful of a Japanese revolt and a resumption of hostilities.

escaped into the country and continued to fight in pockets of resistance until the end of the war.

Iwo Jima was the next key island in the race across the Pacific. It was only eight square miles of volcanic rock and ash, but it was defended by 20,000 Japanese soldiers. The battle was murderous. The defenders had pulled back from the beaches, but were well dug-in inland. The terrain was difficult for both men and equipment. It took almost a month to plant the American flag on Mount Suribachi.

However, it was yet another stepping stone. If Japan was to be successfully invaded, the much bigger island of Okinawa would have to be captured to provide the base for an attack. Okinawa had well over 100,000 defenders and a significant number of planes, including *Kamikaze* units. *Kamikaze* attacks had inflicted heavy losses and were almost impossible to defend against. They struck fear into the Americans, who found them alien and horrifying. The battle for Okinawa was the zenith of the *Kamikaze* tradition. They sank 30 warships and damaged hundreds more. Not only were the attacks themselves damaging and demoralizing to the Americans, they also reinforced the belief that the Japanese would not surrender their homeland under any circumstances.

The attack on Okinawa began on 1 April 1945 and, to the shock of the Americans, met with no resistance for five days. But then, the Japanese launched a massive onslaught. They even committed their biggest battleship, the fabled *Yamato,* in a naval assault, despite the

ABOVE: Filming secret US atomic tests in the desert.

fact that it hadn't enough fuel to return from the engagement. It was, in effect, a suicide mission. On land, the Japanese defenders hid in caves or bunkers and had to be blown up by grenades or incinerated by flame-throwers to end their resistance. The capture of the island cost over 12,000 American lives and over 110,000 Japanese. The *Kamikaze* did their worst. In one attack, 355 pilots swooped at once. They all perished in return for five American ships.

In May, Rangoon fell to the British army and mainland Japan was in the grip of merciless heavy bombing from B-29 'Superfortresses'. Tokyo was all but razed to the ground. Nagoya, Osaka and Kobe all suffered similar fates. The Japanese army was gradually losing control in China and, by August, fighting had already

broken out between Chiang Kai-Shek's nationalists and Mao Tse Tung's communists for the future of the country. Stalin's Red Army was also massing on the border of Manchuria. Japan's position had long been hopeless, but no surrender had yet been offered.

When the American planners considered the options for an invasion of Japan's main islands the predicted death-rates were conservatively projected at tens of thousands of American lives and many times that number of Japanese. To the Americans the losses were unthinkable, but the alternative was also unthinkable.

A month earlier, the first atomic weapon had been tested in the New Mexican Desert. When the director of the project, Robert Oppenheimer, saw the first mushroom cloud, he read from the Hindu saga, *Bhagavad Gita:* 'I am become Death, the shatterer of worlds.'

By the time it came to make the decision to use the weapon, British Prime Minister Winston Churchill had lost the post-war general election and had been replaced by Clement Attlee. Although Churchill had already endorsed its use, Truman stood alone in making the decision. A final demand for unconditional surrender was issued to the Japanese on 26 July. It was rejected two days later.

The atomic bomb was dropped twice: once on Hiroshima on 6 August and once on Nagasaki on 9 August. The consequences shook the world. At least 80,000 were killed in Hiroshima and at least 40,000 in Nagasaki. Although many more had died elsewhere, even in a single night of bombing, nothing had prepared the world for the horror that could now be unleashed, in an instant, by a single bomb.

It was Emperor Hirohito who finally made the decision to surrender. He remained on the throne and made the announcement to his people by radio on 15 August, the first time the nation had ever heard his voice.

The formal surrender was signed on the American battleship, *USS Missouri,* in Tokyo Bay, two weeks later.

The Second World War was over.

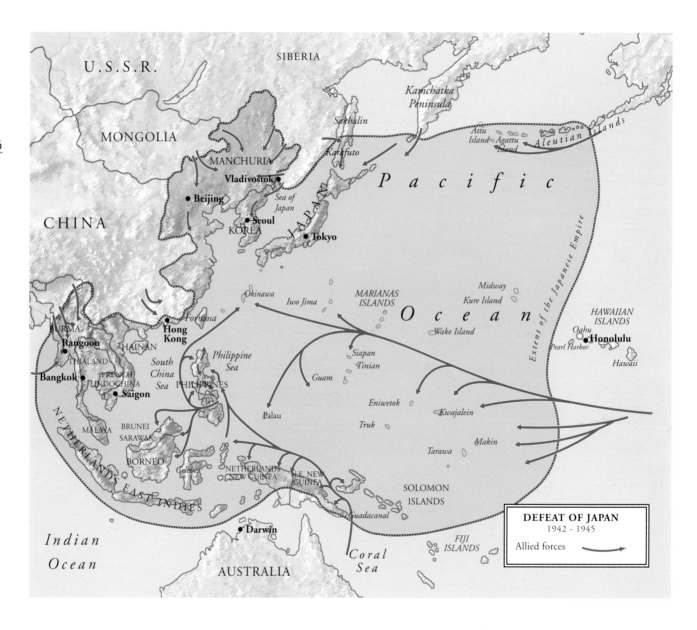

ABOVE: The tide turned for Japan in the Pacific as relentlessly as it turned for its Axis partners in Europe. When the Marianas Islands fell, Japan was vulnerable to America's massive air power.

CHRONOLOGY: JANUARY–SEPTEMBER 1945

1945

Jan. 1 US forces take Mindoro in the Philippines.

Feb. 3 The month-long American siege of Manila begins.

Feb. 4 Low-level incendiary bombing raids begin on Japan.

Feb. 19 The American assault on the Japanese island of Iwo Jima begins.

Mar. 20 British and Indian troops in Burma reach Mandalay.

Apr. 1 The three-month battle for Okinawa begins.

May 4 Rangoon is captured by the Allies.

July 5 The Philippines are finally liberated from Japan.

Aug. 3 Fighting breaks out between the nationalists and the communists in China.

Aug. 6 The first atomic bomb is dropped on Hiroshima.

Aug. 8 The Soviets declare war on Japan and invade Manchuria.

Aug. 9 The second atomic bomb is dropped on Nagasaki.

Aug. 12 The Red Army occupies North Korea.

Aug. 14 It is announced that Emperor Hirohito will surrender under Allied terms. His radio broadcast takes place the following day.

Sep. 2 The formal Japanese surrender is signed on the USS *Missouri*.

5 December 1944 – Letter from Shihoko Katoh, a Japanese schoolgirl

Letter found on the body of Kanichi Horimoto the pilot of the suicide plane that, at dawn on 4 May 1945, attacked the USS Ingraham *near Okinawa.*

To a brave warrior of the Divine Eagles

The aspects of the war have been getting more and more intense. We have no words to express our gratitude to a god of the Divine Eagles, a Special Attack Corps, who will go to the front for the decisive battle. Please beat the hell out of the hated Americans and British with peace in mind and without worrying about the future. We are putting all of our forward efforts into [war] production with the 'never-cease-attacking' spirit of the Kamikaze Special Attack Corps until the Great Japanese Empire will be crowned with victory.

December 5 [1944]

Class 3, Year 1 Tokyo Public Sakuramachi Women's High School Katoh, Shihoko

The campaign in Burma was one of the longest and bloodiest of the war. General Slim's Allied army was predominantly Indian, but included British, Gurkha, Chinese, Burmese and African troops.

––––––––

Allied casualties during the campaign numbered over 70,000 (over 6,000 killed). Japanese casualties numbered over 100,000 (over 16,000 killed).

Saturday, 28 April 1945 – A Soldier in the Russian Army

A letter sent by a Soviet soldier from Berlin to his mother on the situation in the captured city.

Russian Army, Soviet Sector, Berlin, Germany

Dear Mother,

All the great and unprecedented things which I witnessed these days will be imprinted in my memory forever.

This letter was written in Berlin. Yes, it is no dream, no gibberish, no fantasy, but the very reality. In Berlin.

It is difficult to realize this is true, but your eyes and ears confirm the reality which your brain cannot accept. I entered Berlin for the first time at 9 in the morning of April 23. … Hastily written slogans in German on the fences, reflecting the moment – 'Berlin will remain German' etc. (what an irony – all German spells and prophecies are blowing up like a soap bubble).

[…]

Women, men and children were coming by and asking for bread, for something to eat, shamelessly, with a hungry glow in their eyes, with forced pathetic smiles. I have involuntary tears in my eyes even now, when I remember this. It was a sad procession of hungry and frightened people.

Then the Berlin population started to rob the shops. The crowd

BELOW: A mushroom cloud billows into the sky above Nagasaki.

RIGHT: *The barren landscape that was once the bustling Japanese city of Hiroshima.*

The 'chindits' was the name given to Orde Wingate's 'Long Range Penetration' groups, which fought in the Burma campaign. The name derives from 'chintha', the Burmese name for the unit's insignia, the winged lions which guard Buddhist temples.

On the heaviest night of bombing over Tokyo, on the night of 9/10 March 1945, 334 B-29 Superfortresses created a firestorm which killed almost 100,000 people and practically levelled the city.

pressed in through broken shop windows and doors. Old men staggered under the burden of sacks with food, old women snatched cans from children.

[…] Tram wires in the street were torn down somewhere, and white Berlin trams stood immobile where the tide of war had left them.

MONDAY, 6 AUGUST 1945 – ZENJI ORITA

In 1941, Zenji Orita was second in command of a Japanese submarine that participated in the Japanese attack on the US fleet anchored in Pearl Harbor. By August 1945 he had become an instructor at a Navy submarine school at Otake near Hiroshima.

JAPANESE NAVY, OTAKE, JAPAN

Then came Aug. 6, the day when 'two suns', one natural and the other manmade, cast their fiery glow over Hiroshima, not very far from my place of duty. An air raid warning sounded at 8 a.m. at Otake, but I did not pay much attention to it. There were false alarms and the radio at the time was reporting that only one lone B-29 had been sighted in the sky. I gathered up my books and was about to head for my classroom when, at about 8.15 a.m. a terrific explosion was heard. A short time later, all the windows on the north side of my building were blown in by an air blast, the great pressure wave emanating from where an atomic bomb was first dropped on human beings. I looked toward Hiroshima. A large cloud was spreading over the city. It then seemed to zoom upwards with ever-increasing speed, after which it topped off at a great height, giving it the appearance of a giant mushroom.

[...]

Whenever my glance moved in the direction of Hiroshima that day, I was thankful that none of my family, relatives or friends lived there.

TUESDAY, 14 AUGUST 1945 – JOAN VEAZEY

VJ Day as seen by Mrs Veazey.

ENGLAND

It has been wonderful to watch the end of this dreadful war. And now that we have France, there will be no more fears ... of being blown to pieces, by bombs or being burnt alive by fire in our homes, at least we will now sleep at nights! As soon as we can get our men home, there will be great joy for those who left their loved ones behind. Some, many, will never return – those who have been lost in this awful fight, we owe our peace to them ... as well as those who have been saved. In honour of those – who have not returned, I pray that one day the World will forget its selfishness and greed, its love of money and longing for the less work. Then maybe their sacrifice will not be in vain.

As long as we go on inventing and making new and more deadly weapons of War and destruction we shall be tempted to use them. It is for the scientists to use their brains to help in healing ... to make machines to help heal, rather than to maim and kill. If they don't do this, then the Mothers of all the lands will cry out 'God Save our Children'.

TUESDAY, 4 SEPTEMBER 1945 – GUNNER BOB GRAFTON

Gunner Bob Grafton was a prisoner of war in the Far East from 1942 to 1945. In Burma he was forced to work on the construction of the Burma–Siam railway. This letter to his teenage sweetheart, Dorothy, was written soon after he was liberated.

My dear Dorothy,

This is my first letter as a free man. I am devoting it to you darling as I know how much our thoughts are the same at the moment. With this letter starts a new life for both of us. Here too starts the realisation of the dreams which for me, seemed too far away to ever come true. Yet, although our first weeks of freedom have been very quiet and uneventful because we have not fully realised that we are free we are as patient as ever. [...]

The atomic bomb dropped on Hiroshima was a uranium bomb nicknamed 'Little Boy'. The Nagasaki bomb was a plutonium boy called 'Fat Boy'. The losses in each city were fewer than the Dresden or Tokyo firestorms.

At the end of the war the five major protagonists (USA, USSR, Germany, Japan and Britain) had (respectively) 14.8, 11.2, 9.1, 5.3 and 5.0 million men under arms (45.4 million total).

————

Of the estimated total of 50 million war dead between 1939 and 1945, 22 million are thought to have been military casualties, 28 million are thought to have been civilians.

ABOVE: The aftermath of an American bombing raid on a Japanese submarine pen.

RIGHT: The Official Japanese surrender aboard the USS Missouri, 2 September 1945.

But sweetheart, thankfully I believe I'm much fitter, stronger and more of a man for the experience than when I kissed you goodbye on the station in August, 1941. The next kiss will be the first since so watch out darling! I dreamed of you many, many times and such places, but the dreams always ended in my having to return to the hell on earth. It won't be like that […]

I still have tons to say and so little space every word is precious! Disappointing only room to say it briefly when I want to so much I love you, I love you, I think that you are the most courageous having waited so long.

Goodnight darling, Tons of love and kisses

BOB

SUNDAY, 10 FEBRUARY 1946 – ROSEY NORWALK

Before returning to the United States Rosey visited occupied Europe. Below she describes a dinner she had while in the German town of Dachau.

JOURNAL, MUNICH, GERMANY

Just sent off a long letter to Bob about having dinner at the Dachau apartment of an American couple who came to Germany for a visit and got caught up here when the war broke out.

Jack, a GI technician and machinist, works with Fred, the American who got caught here with his wife Greta when war broke out.

[…] they came to spend the summer of 1938 in Germany, Fred said, and enjoyed it so much they stayed on for the winter. Yes, they had been very impressed with the new Germany. The cleanliness, the order, the efficiency, the new autobahns with play area for picnicking, the Volkswagens (a nice little car people can afford), young children in uniformed groups hiking over the beautiful countryside, singing as they marched, the value of the German mark after the terrible inflation that followed the Great War. They simply waited too long to apply to return to the States, and then the war caught them.

[…] they had considered becoming Germans again, which is why they stayed on another year. During the war Fred worked a lathe at a small Messerschmitt plant in town, making airplane parts and screws. Yes, there were camp inmates who worked at the plant, hundreds, but they were dirty and sick and not very efficient. They often slumped over their work and the guards dragged them away. They didn't last long. Nazi troopers rode them hard – even the Germans, Fred complained. […]

Greta asked about my Red Cross duties, then told me about her work for the German Red Cross. Said she sewed and made bandages for the wounded – even prisoners, she added proudly – with other women of the town at the home of the camp commandant.

It is estimated that the total number of civilian refugees at the end of the war was thirty million.

RIGHT: Men of the US Army 71st Reconnaissance Group relax on the deck of the SS Cape Victory en route to Seattle from Manila. The war was over.

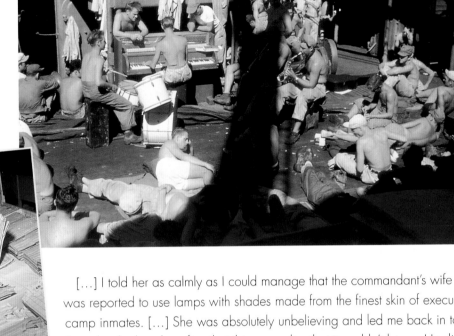

ABOVE: For the British too, life for thousands was to change dramatically. A former serviceman selects clothing with which he was to embark down 'Civvy Street'.

[…] I told her as calmly as I could manage that the commandant's wife was reported to use lamps with shades made from the finest skin of executed camp inmates. […] She was absolutely unbelieving and led me back in to have her husband confirm that this was a lie, that it couldn't be so. He did, of course, and I didn't believe a word […] [Rosey was referring, in fact to the wife of the Buchenwald Camp Commandant Ilse Koch]

He and Greta realised they'd been misled, but there was nothing he could do. […] General Eisenhower ordered all the local citizens to go through the camp. They were forced to help load all the corpses strewn over the camp on wagons. They even had to remove rotting corpses from freight cars sitting at the side gate of the camp. The cars had remained locked in the station for three days after arriving from Buchenwald because the SS fled before the rapidly approaching U.S. troops. The townspeople were ordered to pull the loaded wagons back to town and up the hill, then help dig a pit so the corpses could be buried in the town park that was to become a monument.

'I tried to explain that we were American citizens,' Fred almost sobbed. 'That we were here against our will and not Nazis, that we had no idea conditions were so bad in the camp. But nobody listened and we had to do it. But what could we have done? We had no choice and had to make the best of things. It's been very hard.' […]

On the short ride back to camp […] I did manage a polite goodnight before jumping out of the jeep and running into my quarters. Then I threw up.

NOTES

1 Developed by French artist Jacques Daguerre in 1839. The technique involved the exposure of a silver-coated sheet of copper, treated with iodine vapour to make it light sensitive. Exposures took 15 minutes in bright sunshine. The technique produced a positive image.

2 The Wet-collodion process was introduced by English sculptor F. Scott Archer. Glass plates, coated with collodion (nitrocellulose), were immersed in a silver nitrate solution and exposed in the camera while still wet. The technique necessitated portable darkrooms for photographers working in the field.

3 'Dry-plates' carried a silver halide emulsion in gelatin which meant that the photographers no longer needed to coat and sensitize their plates.

4 The first synthetic plastic material, developed in 1869 by John Lesley Hyatt. Its strength and flexibility were the key to motion imagery.

5 'Magic lantern' methods used drawn images in successive stages of movement, which were then rotated to replicate movement.

6 Edward Muybridge was an English adventurer who sought his fortune in the California Gold Rush of 1849. In 1872, he was recruited by Leland Stanford, the governor of California, to help him win a bet. Stanford had bet a horse-racing rival $25,000 that at some point in a horse's gallop all four of its hooves were clear of the ground. Muybridge rigged twelve cameras on a race track, each one triggered by a wire as the horse galloped by. These successive photographic images were projected by a magic lantern to win Stanford his bet.

7 French inventor Etienne-Jules Marey took his moving images with a single camera in 1882. This technique only allowed a few seconds of movement.

8 The Kinetograph allowed 50 feet of celluloid film to be exposed at 48 frames per second. The images were then projected by another Edison patent, the Kinetoscope, a small 'peep-hole' viewer that could only be viewed by one person at a time. The French Lumiere brothers, Auguste and Louis, developed a machine called a 'Cinematographe' which was much lighter, could be turned by hand and which shot, printed and projected the pictures. Thus, they took the camera from the stage into the outside world.

9 Tinting involved immersing film in dyes to give it a single colour hue.

10 Toning used chemicals to interact with the original film to add a second colour.

11 Kinemacolor was patented in 1906. It involved exposing film at twice the then normal speed, ie. 32 frames per second, rather than 16. During exposure alternate frames were exposed through either a red or green filter. This was reversed on projection. It was used commercially from 1909 and gave an impression of colour.

12 Kodacolor was introduced in 1928, but relied on projection through a colour banded lens system that reinstated the colours from the film's emulsion.

DIARY SOURCES

21, 22, 26, 34, 40 Klemperer, Victor, I Shall Bear Witness (Translated by Martin Chalmers), Wiedenfeld & Nicolson, London 1998

22 von Hassell, Fey, A Mother's War (Edited by David Forbes-Watt), John Murray Ltd, London 1990

23 Thälmann, Ernst, Topography of Terror, Verlag Willmuth Arenhövel

27 Shaporina, Lyubov Vasilievna, (Translated by Caroline Flath), Saltykov-Shchredin Public Library, St Petersburg

28 Greening, Edward Miners, Against Fascism, Hywell Francis 1984

28 Schuschnigg, Kurt von

31 Charlton, Moyra, Imperial War Museum, London

31, 200 Veasey née Wildish, Joan, Imperial War Museum, London

32 Senesh, Hannah, Her Life & Diary (Translated by Martha Cohn), Vallentine, Mitchell, London 1971

37, 40 Sierakowiak, Dawid, Lodz Ghetto (Edited by Alan Adelson and Robert Lapides), Viking Penguin, 1989

38 Philips, Janine, My Secret Diary, Shepheard-Walwyn (Publishers) Ltd, London 1972

38, 46, 56 Shirer, William L, Berlin Diary 1934–1941: The Rise of The Third Reich, Hamish Hamilton, London 1941

41, 70 Last, Nella, Mass Observation, published as Nella Last's War (Edited by Richard Broad and Suzie Fleming), Falling Wall Press, Bristol 1981

48, 50 Brown, Richard, Mr Brown's War (Edited by Helen D Millgate), Sutton Publishing Ltd, Stroud 1998

54, 62, 78 Fuchs, Karl, Sieg Heil!: The Letters of Tank Gunner Karl Fuchs (Edited by Horst Fuchs Richardson) 1987

57 Toomey, Jack, Imperial War Museum by permission of Mrs K Toomey, widow

57 van der Heide, Dirk, My Sister and I (Translated by Mrs Antoon Deventer), Harcourt Brace & Co Inc, New York 1941

68 Perry, Colin, Boy in the Blitz, Leo Cooper Ltd, London 1972

73 Ranfurly, Hermione, Countess of, To War with Whitaker, the Wartime Diaries of the Countess of Ranfurly, Heinemann, London 1994

77 Skriyabina, Elena, Leningrader Tagebuch. Aufzeichnungen aus den Kriegsjahren 1941–45, Wiesbaden, Munchen 1985

77 Rubinowicz, Dawid, The Diary of Dawid Rubinowicz (Translated by Derek Bowman), Blackwood Press, Edinburgh, 1981

77, 117 Colville, Sir John, The Fringes of Power, 10 Downing St Diaries, 1939–1955, Hodder & Stoughton Ltd, London 1985

79 Rolnikas, Macha, Je Devais le Raconter (Translated by Christine Lienhart Nelson), Les Editeurs Francais Reunis, Paris 1966

82 Goebbels, Paul Joseph

83 Amosoff, Nikolai, Mikhailovich, PPG-2266: A Surgeon's War, Henry Regnery & Co, Chicago 1975

84, 175, 176 Morell, Theodor, *The Secret Diaries of Hitler's Doctor*, (Edited by David Irvine), Sidgewick and Jackson, London 1983

91 Rupp, Karl, *German War Against the Soviet Union, 1941–45*. The documentary exhibition.

91 Volkov, Volodya, *German War Against the Soviet Union, 1941–45*. The documentary exhibition.

92 Prüller, Wilhelm, *Diary of A German Soldier*, (Translated by H C Robbins Landom), Coward-McCann, New York 1963

94 Scott, Michael, Imperial War Museum, London

101 Lewis, John, *Joy Street: A Wartime Romance in Letters* (Edited by Michael T Wise), Little, Brown & Co., New York, 1995

102 Heidt, Wesley John, USS *Arizona* Memorial Museum, US National Parks Service

103 Tufteland, Raymond, Mr Raymond F Tufteland

103 Sakamaki, Kazuo, US National Archives and Records Administration

106 Wyatt, John, Imperial War Museum by permission of Mr John Wyatt

109 Rudashevski, Yitshok, *The Diary of The Vilna Ghetto: June 1941–April 1943* Translated by Percy Matenko, Ghetto Fighter's House, Israel 1973

109 Konstantinova, Ina, *The Girl From Kashin*, Komsommol Press, Moscow, 1947. Reprinted and translated by Jean Cottam in 'The Girl From Kashin' MA/AH Publishing, Manhattan, KS

110, 111 Unknown Japanese Soldiers, US National Archives & Records Administration

111 Perazzo, G, Australian War Memorial

116 Milburn, Clara Emily, *Mrs Milburn's Diaries*, (Edited by Peter Donnelly), George G. Harrap, London 1979

120 Curry, Frank, *Veterans' Affairs*, Canada website

124 Lewin, Abraham, *A Cup of Tears: The Journal of Abraham Lewin* 1988

124 Adams, Milton, *Taps For A Jim Crow Army* (Edited by Philip McGuire), 1983

126, 168, 175 Frank, Anne, (Edited by Otto H Frank & Mirjam Pressler, translated Susan Massotty), Anne Frank-Fonds, Basel 1991/Doubleday, London, 1995

129, 130, 169, 172, 179, 184, 202 Norwalk, Rosey, *Dearest Ones: A True World War II Love Story*, John Wiley & Sons Inc, New York 1999

141 Berg, Mary

149 Knoke, Heinz, *I Flew for the Fuehrer: The Story of A German Airman*, (Translated by John Ewing), Evans Bros Ltd, London 1953

149 Goldman, Carl, *Jewish Youth: Letters from American Soldiers*, J Rontch, 1945

152, 157 Solomon, Sam, *Jewish Youth: Letters from American Soldiers*, J Rontch, 1945

154 Branson, Clive, *British Soldier in India: The Letters of Clive Branson*, London, 1944

159 Kuribayashi, Tadamichi, Mr Taro Kuribayashi

166 Hughes, GE, Imperial War Museum, London

169 Rowberry, Ivor, *Tatler & Bystander*, 18th September, 1946, Imperial War Museum by permission of Miss Patricia Rowberry, sister

173 Peterson, Leslie R, The Jeffrey L Ethell Collection

176 The Unknown Brother and Sister of Lodz Ghetto, 'The Unknown Diarist of Ghetto Lodz', from *Yad Vashem News*, No 2, Israel 1970

177 Leinster, George, Imperial War Museum by permission of Mrs Patricia Leinster, widow

184 Kopelev, Lev

187 Lieber, Leslie, 'What Are the German Civilians Like?', from *Tricolour Magazine*, June, 1945

188 Borkowski, Dieter

189 Koller, Karl, *The Koller War Diary*, (Edited by J Richard Smith), Monogram Aviation Publications, Sturbridge, MA, 1990

190 Rabe, John, *The Good German of Nanking*, Alfred A. Knopf, London 1998

192 Lazerson, Tamarah

198 Katoh, Shihoko, Mr Wesley Fay Hogue

199 Orita, Zenji, I-Boat Captain with Joseph D Harrington, Major Books, Canoga Park, CA 1976

200 Grafton, Bob, Imperial War Museum by permission of Mr Bob Grafton

SELECTED BIBLIOGRAPHY

Ambrose, Stephen, *New History of World War II*, revised and updated, (London 1997). Original text by C.L. Sulzberger.

Beevor, Antony, *Stalingrad* (London 1998).

Bullock, Alan, *Hitler: A Study in Tyranny* (London 1962).

Dear, I.C.B. (ed.), *The Oxford Companion to the Second World War* (Oxford 1995).

Dupuy, R. Ernest and Dupuy, Trevor, *The Collins Encyclopaedia of Military History* (London 1993).

Fest, Joachim, *Plotting Hitler's Death* (London 1996).

Gilbert, Martin, *A History of the Twentieth Century*, Vol. 2 (London 1998).

Grunberger, Richard, *A Social History of the Third Reich* (London 1971).

Keegan, John, *The Second World War*, (London 1990).

Liddell Hart, Basil, *The History of the Second World War* (New York 1971).

Schulze, Hagen, *Germany: A New History* (Cambridge MA 1998).

Shirer, William L., *The Rise and Fall of the Third Reich* (London 1960).

Storry, Richard, *A History of Modern Japan* (London 1960).

Weinberg, Gerhard L., *A World at Arms: A Global History of World War II* (Cambridge 1994).

INDEX

ACKNOWLEDGEMENTS

The authors are grateful to so many people for their support, friendship, knowledge and professionalism in making this project happen, both the book and the ITV series with which it is associated.

At TWI, it could not have happened without the belief and persistence of Michael Mellor and the insight of Alastair Waddington. Michel Masquelier's eloquence in selling the series will ensure that we are not summoned by the company Financial Controller to account for ourselves.

The belief and guidance of our partners at Carlton turned the series from an exciting idea like so many others, into a viable project, like so few. Steve Hewlet, Martin Smith, Polly Bide, Martin Baker, Juliet Lomas and Sian Facer could not have been more professional, nor more helpful. We also owe a particular debt of gratitude to Grant Mansfield, Controller of Documentaries, Features and Arts at ITV Network Centre, who commissioned the series for transmission on ITV. As we finish these acknowledgements, the last thing we write for the book, we will immediately cross our fingers in the hope that we can also help deliver for him a television series which is worthy of his faith in it.

Vivien James, Colin Webb and our editor David Williams at Pavilion Books moved with amazing speed and immense patience to get the book done and presented so well. Our designer Nigel Partridge and map-maker Julian Baker have made the book look much better than the authors deserve.

The TWI production team who are making the ITV series have done all the work to produce the resources upon which this book is based. They are all very talented and dedicated and great people to work with (a nice combination when you can get it!). Lucy Carter, Alastair Laurence, Dunja Noack, Svetlana Palmer, Katie Chadney, Keiko Tanaka, Caroline Osborne, Adam Grint, Sorrel May and Leila Lak should all have been writing the book, had the authors not staked the first claim. We are very grateful to them that they nevertheless let us get on with it and gave us every support.

Several people read our manuscript, helped put some of it into decent English, pointed out our glaring errors and omissions and did whatever they could with clumsy expressions and ponderous style. Taylor Downing, Robert Devine, Christopher Dowling, Terry Charman and Gill Blake did what they could, but don't blame them for what survives.

Finally, our thanks go to Katie Chadney, who helped compile the book from the beginning and prepared the manuscript. Her comments and advice were invaluable.

PICTURE ACKNOWLEDGEMENTS

The publishers would like to thank the following for supplying the images and all copyright holders for permission to reproduce illustrations: AKG, Bildarchiv Preussischer Kulturbesitz, Australian War Memorial, ET Archive, US National Archives, The Jeffrey L Ethell Collection, Jack Havener, Frederick Hill, Richard H Perley, US Air Force Museum, Hulton-Getty, Imperial War Museum, Loecker Verlag, US Library of Congress, US Information Agency.

Every possible effort has been made to trace and acknowledge the copyright holders. However, should any photographs not be correctly attributed, the publisher will undertake any appropriate changes in future editions of the book.
(l = left, r = right, t = top, c = centre, b = bottom)

Imperial War Museum: 1, 14r, 17, 19, 23, 21l, 24t, 26, 29l, 29r, 31, 36, 39l, 39t, 49, 69l, 69t, 74b, 107l, 113, 116r, 119c, 120l, 120b, 120–1c, 122c, 122t, 123l, 123r, 128b, 128t, 129l, 129r, 131l, 134, 135, 138–9, 147l, 147r, 150t, 150–1, 152l, 152r, 152–3, 154l, 156, 158, 159, 167, 169, 170, 181, 193b, 193t, 203l Imperial War Museum; 9, 13 IWM/Lt Len Chetwyn; 14l IWM/Lt Gade.

AKG: 3, 10, 14c, 27, 52c; 52lr; 52tl; 52tr; 56l; 56–7, 60, 70, 71, 79l, 85, 143r, 145l; 58l, 59l, 61 AKG/Official German Military Photo; 68 AKG/WE Frh v Medem; 76–7, 80, 81, 91, 108–9 AKG/Grimm; 93 AKG/Henrich; 105b AKG/WE Frh v Medem; 106 AKG/Rieder; 142 AKG/Sturm; 145r, 146l AKG/Ernst Franck.

Jeffrey L Ethell Collection: 118–19, 119t, 131t, 133b, 136, 148b, 148t, 149, 150b, 151t, 171t, 188, 191t; 8 Ethell/Jack K Havener; 11, 104, 114, 125, 152, 154r, 157t, 166, 171b, 172, 173b, 173t, 174t, 186l, 189t, 190b, 192c, 192b, 192t, 194, 195, 198 Ethell/US National Archives; 12 Ethell/JK Havener; 97 Ethell/USIA; 132l, 132–3 Ethell/Frederick Hill; 132t Ethell/John Quincy/Stanley Wyglendowski; 148c Ethell/US Air Force Museum; 179, 203r Ethell/Hill; 184 Ethell/Richard H Perley.

Bildarchiv Preussischer Kulturbesitz: 30l, 43, 44, 51, 74tl, 74–5, 83, 110b; 30t, 58r, 59t BPK/Official German Military Photo; 34–5 BPK/Karl Heinrich Paulmann; 62, 63 BPK/Heinrich Hoffman; 65, 79t, 110t BPK/H Hoeffke; 87 BPK/Hans Hubmann.

ET Archive: 80t, 116l, 122b, 143l, 157b, 191b; 53, 73 ETA/Australian War Memorial; 96, 105t, 160, 162, 174b, 185b, 186r, 189b, 190t, 199, 201b, 201t ETA/US National Archives; 184–5 ETA/IWM.

Hulton Getty: 72b, 72t, 107r, 117l, 117r, 119b.

Loecker Verlag: 86, 89l, 89l, 89r.

Jacket credits: *Front:* l ETA/US National Archives; c Ethell/US National Archives; r Ethell/US National Archives; *Back:* cr BPK; lc BPK/Heinrich Hoffman; bl AKG/Grimm; tc IWM; tl IWM; tr Ethell/Frederick Hill